I0214609

Modernism and Mildred Walker

Modernism and Mildred Walker

Carmen Pearson

University of Nebraska Press
Lincoln and London

Publication of this volume was assisted by a grant from Mount Royal College.

Manufactured in the United States of America
∞

Library of Congress Cataloging-in-Publication Data
Pearson, Carmen A.
Modernism and Mildred Walker / Carmen Pearson.
p. cm.
Includes bibliographical references and index.
ISBN 978-0-8032-3760-5 (cloth : alk. paper)
1. Walker, Mildred, 1905–1998—Criticism and interpretation.
2. Modernism (Literature)—United States. I. Title.
PS3545.A524Z84 2008
813'.52—dc22
2007045206

Set in Quadraat & Quadraat Sans by Bob Reitz.
Designed by R. W. Boeche.

p. iii: Mildred Walker. Photo courtesy of Christopher M. Schemm.

Contents

Preface

I first came across Mildred Walker's work in the fall of 1995. At the time, I was snowbound in Great Falls, Montana, having traveled down from Canada to pick up a load of ponies. An early winter storm had blown in that day, and I found myself wandering around a bookstore trying to find a distraction from thoughts of the trip I had just made, of slipping and sliding in the ruts of semis with a rented horse trailer blowing back and forth. Since I'd been traveling through winter wheat country all afternoon—as best as I could tell in the drifting snow—the title of Mildred Walker's recently republished book, *Winter Wheat*, caught my eye.

The next morning, with the snow replaced by ferocious winds, I found my way to Curtis Lee's little farm on the banks of the Missouri River to pick up his band of Shetlands. The vivid landscape of Walker's book shadowed my thoughts as I helped load the little animals. Curtis was selling his farm and taking the proceeds to move into a nursing home. It was all a little sad—him showing me photos and trophies from Great Falls' fairs in the 1940s and '50s. On that day I had no idea that almost fifteen years later I'd find myself less than a mile from his place, again standing on the banks of the Missouri, again in Great Falls, again picking up something and hauling it home, and I had no idea that the book I'd bought the night before just to lull myself to sleep would have something to do with it all.

Like Mary Clearman Blew, the little girl who realized for the first time that lives like hers were worth writing about when she found a copy of *The Curlew's Cry* in a local Montana library, I too was happy to realize that the seemingly mundane and backwater existence I lived was somehow validated in words—beautiful words. Subsequently, I arranged to have each new reissue of Walker's novels by the University of Nebraska Press sent to our farm in Alberta. Certainly, my initial enthusiasm for Walker's fiction was by no means scholarly. It was entirely personal, and probably still is. Her settings were realistic, as were her characters. Her books didn't have happy endings. They just stopped because there wasn't anything else to say. Her characters and writing had an integrity that I valued. So with just that, I sent copies of her books to my family and friends and carried on in my little backwater, secretly wishing I could meet the author. But, like many things, I waited too long—or so I thought.

As with many mothers and wives, my life changed when my husband came home one day, and although I did not know it at the time, the news that Andrew announced would bring me a whole lot closer to meeting Mildred Walker than I could have ever imagined. He explained that he had been offered a job in Houston and thought it would be nice to have a break from Alberta's winter and snow, just for a season or two, and he asked what we thought. Initially, we were horrified. We had horses, sheep, chickens—not exactly a mobile group—and I sure wasn't a "trailing spouse." But we struck a compromise. My husband was itching for a little change, we'd find someone to stay at the farm, and hadn't I always vowed that when I was old, I'd finish my PhD? Maybe this was the opportunity, I reasoned.

I discovered that not many universities are interested in a middle-aged mamma who wants to pursue a PhD in English, having no formal education in the subject. However, luck was on my side. With characteristic Southern hospitality, the University of Houston didn't slam their door but instead said they'd give me a chance to see what I could do. Well, I knew how to read and how to work. With little else than that, I started. They let me stay. When it came time to pick a subject for a dissertation, I was still feeling pretty insecure, an outsider to the inner sanctums of English academia. Maybe because of this—or despite it—I carried my collection of Walker's books into the university and announced that I would like to write about Mildred Walker. Other students were doing Shakespeare and Virginia Woolf. Although I was green behind the ears and already figured most people had never heard of her, I wasn't all that green—but of course, I only realize that now.

Even though it did not include much formal literary training, my upbringing had given me a postmodern sensibility, whether I knew it or not. I would like to believe this had something to do with living in the West. Instinctively, I sensed that what happened out West was just as relevant to a fuller understanding of American culture as what occurred other places. I also knew that certain stories and voices had been sidelined for too many years and that something needed to be done about it. Of course, I wasn't alone in my opinion. Others—esteemed scholars of American literature—felt the same way. Members of the Western Literature Association had been dropping hints for years that someone ought to give more critical attention to Mildred Walker. The proof was also in the publication record; the University of Nebraska Press had dedicated considerable resources to bringing Walker's books back into print. If they were worth reading, surely they were also worth studying. I felt I was the one for the job.

As I embarked on my dissertation, it didn't hurt that Ladette Randolph at the University of Nebraska Press had already offered her encouragement and that Ripley Hugo, Mildred Walker's daughter and biographer, was already helping me in every way she could. If the heavens line up in a certain way on a specific day and they let you pass through, you take that as a good sign. Nervously, I went to one of the faculty members at the University of Houston, Dr. Dorothy Baker, to ask her if she would supervise my dissertation. To my surprise, she had attended Walker's alma mater, Wells College, and had colleagues who had known Walker. Dr. Baker agreed to the project. This coincidence fueled my sense of fate and I continued on.

The road to completing my PhD—like that snowy road from Lethbridge to Shelby—had a few blind spots, bends, and surprises. But, in the end, I'm back at the farm and it all worked out just fine. Along the way, I discovered that Walker had left one manuscript for a novel unpublished. Working with Ripley via phone and mail, I edited *The Orange Tree* for posthumous publication before completing this critical study. Editing the manuscript set me back in terms of time but not in learning. Walker left several versions of the manuscript, and for the better part of one winter, I sat in my office in the barn and studied her notes and words, talked to her ghost, and tried to understand how she created a novel. This experience, along with long phone conversations and letters from Ripley, helped me through the project. Of all the fine English teachers I have had, Walker proved to be the best. If you admire a writer, sitting and rewriting and editing his or her every single word is a journey you should take. But my journey didn't end there. I was fortunate enough to visit Walker's former home in Grafton, Vermont. Christopher and Deniza Schemm, Walker's youngest son and daughter-in-law, were exemplary hosts, inviting me to their home and kind enough even to house me in what had been Mildred's room. On that visit, we walked to the local cemetery, sat on the edge of the Saxtons River, and hiked through the woods, searching for the erratic boulder featured in *A Piece of the World* and the overgrown quarries depicted in *The Quarry*. I also peeked around a traditional New England house, complete with a separate wing, as memorialized in *The Southwest Corner*. Again, in Oregon, George and Janet Schemm allowed me to sleep in a wing of their beautiful home when I came to visit. I didn't sleep as much as I should have though, because the room contained what was left of Walker's private collection of books. In short, everything to do with the work of Walker was an adventure and a huge treat—and I've come to the conclusion that that is what real education should be.

Ironically, of all the people who helped me write this book, I have not yet personally met perhaps the most important one. Maybe I have not yet made the shortest trip—to Missoula—because, like her mother, Ripley Hugo's spirit and intelligence sparkle in her words so much that I felt as though I had met her from our first telephone conversation. From the start, she has been the kind and intelligent voice across the line. She is the one who gave me directions to her family home, Beaverbank, on the banks of the Missouri, that beautiful September day when I walked just downstream from the spot where Curtis Lee had given me his ponies many years earlier. She is the careful editor—the one who sent me notes and letters. She gave the most, and I hope that what follows is worthy of your efforts, Ripley. We have both said we would meet someday, and that our meeting has to be at Tupa—and I hope we will.

Of all Walker's residences, Tupa, the family cabin in the Sawtooth Mountains, was one of her favorites. In *Unless the Wind Turns*, her character's description of a cabin certainly expresses her own feelings: "This cabin's mine. [. . .] A place that you keep going back to in your life is always more than a place. It's a kind of measuring ground and a philosophy and a hide-out" (182).

My work with Mildred Walker has also been a measuring ground. Through her novels, with their vivid examples of the integrity and artistry of ordinary people, and the hospitality of her kind and generous offspring, I have gone on an incredible journey that will always be my benchmark. It was a journey fueled by words, like Walker's own life. For this reason I chose to discuss her work within the context of modernism. Although, as the following pages will demonstrate, many critical approaches are apt for studying Walker's work, modernism's distinguishing characteristic is that meaning and art are found not only in the stories, the struggles, the characters, and the landscapes, but in the creation of the words themselves. When taken alone, the subjects of Walker's novels—economics, war, motherhood, aesthetics—give little indication of how her books fit in the modernist tradition. Novels have always been about love, money, wars, family relationships, and historical events. What distinguishes modernist fiction such as Walker's is that a novel is written not simply to entertain or inform but to sanctify the very act of writing.

There are areas of this study that could have been expanded, and I hope that someday soon other scholars will study Walker's fiction and do so. For instance, the relationship between modernism and westering and Walker's focus on relationships, the nuclear family, and complex female characters are topics that deserve more detailed study. Likewise, with the growing interest in eco-criticism, Walker's attention to the relationship between landscape and cultural production lends itself to detailed eco-critical study. It is my hope that this initial study might encourage such work.

Acknowledgments

I wish to offer a special thanks to the University of Nebraska Press and its staff for republishing Mildred Walker's novels for the public—without its efforts, I would never have discovered her works—and to the many individuals behind the scenes who are responsible for this study, particularly Louis Welch for passing my initial questions on to Ripley Hugo. Again, I must thank UNP for publishing Ripley Hugo's biography of her mother, *Writing for Her Life: The Novelist Mildred Walker*. Without this carefully researched and well-presented text coupled with Ripley's personal and always generous guidance, information, and advice, this project never could have even been initiated. Furthermore, Ripley's introducing me to her brothers and their families has enriched both this project and my life. Deniza and Christopher Schemm, I wish to thank you for those special days in Grafton, looking for the erratic boulder and the long-lost quarries and meeting your friends and family. George and Janet, thank you for our evening in Oregon and for my night with all of Mildred's books.

The encouragement and support of many individuals have been integral to this project, most notably that of Ripley Hugo and her family and Ladette Randolph and other members of the UNP staff. Thank you to Christopher Steinke and Joeth Zucco for your careful editorial work. The librarians, archivists, and staff at the American Heritage Center at the University of Wyoming supported this project with both the use of their archives and a travel grant. Early publications of material on this project by the *South Dakota Review*, *Western American Literature*, and *Legacy*, coupled with invitations to present papers on Mildred Walker at conferences held by the Western Literature Association, the Society for the Study of American Women Writers, the American Literature Association, and the Association for the Study of Literature and the Environment provided further encouragement in this work, as did the supportive and helpful critiques of both Ann Ronald and Mary Clearman Blew.

The educational guidance and support of the faculty of English at the University of Houston, particularly that of Dr. Dorothy Baker, Dr. Maria González, Dr. Irving Rothman, and Dr. Linda Westervelt, have been instrumental in this project. A special thanks to Dr. Steven Mintz for his service as an outside reader and to Dr. James Kastely, who smoothed the often riddled course of graduate studies. Additionally, thanks to the women's studies department at the University of Houston for their generous award and encouragement of my work on Mildred Walker. Also, thanks to all the administrative staff behind the scenes at the university, library, and various offices that assisted me with this project. A special thanks goes to the journal *Legacy: A Journal of American Women Writers* (vol. 22, no. 2 [2005]) for giving permission to reprint a version of my profile of Mildred Walker in the introductory material of this text.

Introduction

The purpose of this study is to offer the first comprehensive critical reading of the major fictional works of Mildred Walker. Its goals are to suggest a variety of interpretations that will encourage readers already familiar with Walker's novels to reevaluate her works and their implications and also to encourage new readers and students of literature to undertake further critical studies of the author's fiction. The study's methodology will be to evaluate the author's novels in light of critical concerns that have previously been, and are currently, discussed in the context of modernism. In doing so, a further goal of this study is to reiterate and reinforce the value of what Hugh Witemeyer, in *The Future of Modernism*, refers to as a postmodern version of modernist criticism and to contribute to the ongoing reevaluation of modernism as a critical idiom.

Walker's life spanned the twentieth century, from 1905 to 1998, and her literary production lasted almost three-quarters of a century. Eleven of her novels were first published with Harcourt Brace between 1934 and 1970. Her last published novel was *A Piece of the World*, a work of young adult fiction published by Atheneum Press in 1971. All these novels were out of print in 1992, when the University of Nebraska Press reissued *Winter Wheat*. Subsequent to that publication, all her previously published novels have been reissued to the public under the press's Bison imprint. Moreover, in 2006 the University of Nebraska

Press posthumously released her last novel, *The Orange Tree.*

With a new reading public and an extensive body of readily available literature to draw upon, Walker's place in and contribution to American letters deserve greater critical understanding and appreciation. The biggest challenge to presenting the initial critical study of Walker's collected works is in choosing a critical idiom that not only does justice to the author's diverse works and interests but also encourages future studies that may lead students and readers to a variety of interpretations, something that her works are certainly conducive to. With the diversity of fresh approaches evident in the new critical introductions included in the reissues, certainly what can be agreed upon is that Walker's engagement and concern with the issues of her time are still relevant today.

Modernism is an appropriate critical idiom for an examination of Walker's work because it encourages readings that take into account the times in which she lived, her many areas of interest, and the stylistic adaptations that she exhibited over her long career as a writer. Furthermore, in light of critics' and scholars' reevaluations and discussions of modernism in recent years and the ongoing interest in modernism, this study addresses these developments in order to reevaluate modernism in a postmodern light.

Modernism is no longer defined solely by avant-garde aesthetic reactions to modernity in the first half of the twentieth century, when Walker produced much of her work, but is increasingly thought of as a multicultural, philosophical, and social reaction that emerged in many forms in response to the vast changes sweeping through the modern world that altered the public's perception of what was once considered stable and predictable. Although this study will consider the various definitions of modernism and the different forms it took in Europe, the United States, and the rest of the world, the text's focus will be on the author's reactions to the era in which she lived and her contributions to modernist American literature.

In particular, this study will address the cultural issues raised in the novels: human relationships, family dynamics, the changing roles for women and children in our society and in fiction, the movement of the population from the East to the West, the effect of an evolving U.S. economy on its communities, the many cultural faces of the U.S. population, the integrity and importance of the natural world, and literature's place in that world. I also focus on the importance of "readerly" interpretations of modernist texts through the use of unreliable narrators, changing points of view, and poetic techniques such as the extended metaphor and literary compression.

Not only was modernism a movement in which literature opened to readers in a new way, allowing and encouraging readerly participation in the creative process, it was also a period of time when technology, capitalism, and the American artist seemed to come together for a brief and gilded hour. During the 1920s, '30s, and '40s, before the well-paid and recognized in America consisted mainly of football players and rock stars, writers and other artists were among America's first celebrities. Writers such as John Steinbeck, F. Scott Fitzgerald, and Ernest Hemingway were well-compensated for their work and were recognized by wide audiences, as were many other authors who are not as well-known to today's readers. With a public that read and a publishing industry that had finally come into its own, before the advent of TV and computers and the many competing public media we have today, the *Book of the Month Club* selections and magazines such as the *Atlantic Monthly*, *Scribner's*, *Redbook*, and the *Saturday Evening Post* were integral to the entertainment and educational process in many homes.

In the Mildred Walker Archives at the University of Wyoming, the carefully folded *Book of the Month Club* selections and issues of *New York Times Book Review* featuring her novels are evidence of those special days as are comments in her journals describing her excitement over a release of a new novel and how "royally" her publishers treated her. This period of celebrity for modernist writers is also one of the factors that distinguishes modernism from postmodernism.

American modernist publications were not limited to the U.S. audience in their readership or their subject matter. American fiction had truly become international; particularly with the rise of expatriate writers, U.S. fiction moved, both physically and spiritually, beyond the borders of North America. After two world wars, with rapidly changing technology contributing to less expensive modes of transportation, the earth became smaller and globalization shifted into overdrive. The world's nations became more interested in one another. Even an author from Great Falls, Montana, had her novels translated into nine other languages and toured Europe to visit foreign publishers. Evidence of this internationalization of American literature can also be found in samples of letters from her foreign readers, from soldiers stationed abroad, and even from a young teacher in Japan. Accordingly, this work addresses international issues that indicate the increasingly globalized perspective in American literature.

With the exception of Ripley Hugo's biography of her mother, *Writing for Her Life: The Novelist Mildred Walker*, no text has been fully dedicated to a study of Walker or her novels. Hugo's biography presents invaluable critical information concerning her mother's fiction and brings attention both to the events in Walker's life that influenced the settings, characters, and themes in her novels and to the concerns and beliefs that contributed to her development as a novelist. Hugo's integration of setting, personal details of her mother's life, and an analysis of the texts' creation influences the approach of this study. This work aims not to study literature in isolation from its source of creation and reception but rather to present an integrated discussion focusing on the cultural and social histories and background of the texts, their authors' personal experiences and inspirations for their creation, and readers' reactions to the texts. In this light, *Modernism and Mildred Walker* responds to Ripley Hugo's biography and should be viewed as a continuation of *Writing for Her Life*.

Of all her literary works, *Winter Wheat* has received the most critical attention. However, to date, much of this attention has focused on the novel's setting in Montana, its realistic depictions of western life, and its contribution to the region's literary heritage. With the exception of Elaine Jahner, in her *Spaces of the Mind: Narrative and Community in the American West*, critics have not focused on the novel's complexity and success as a literary work. Jahner dedicates several chapters to a detailed discussion of *Winter Wheat* through discourse theory. Her study encourages critical approaches to the fiction of Walker that blend a use of regionalism with a fresh approach to formalism. In other recent works that discuss her novels, writers most often highlight the need for more critical work on her fiction. These include William Bevis's *Ten Tough Trips: Montana Writers and the West*; Mary Clearman Blew's *Bone Deep in Landscape: Writing, Reading, and Place*; Krista Comer's *Landscapes of the New West: Gender and Geography in Contemporary Women's Writing*; Ken Egan Jr.'s *Hope and Dread in Montana Literature*, William Kittredge and Annick Smith's *The Last Best Place: A Montana Anthology*, and Ann Ronald's *Reader of the Purple Sage*.

Because the term "modernism" and the approaches to this critical idiom are so contentious, a separate chapter is dedicated to modernism's historical context, its various uses as a term, and a suggested definition in light of recent critical discussions. The definition formulated in this chapter attempts to bridge the aesthetic interests of formalists and New Critics, characterized by their interest in high modernism's poetry, with postmodernists' inclination for approaching literary criticism with intertextual, multidisciplinary, and multicultural studies. The conclusion of the discussion is that both approaches can and ought to be wed.

Modernist texts, as Matthew Bruccoli describes them in *Ernest Hemingway and the Expatriate Modernist Movement*, are both "diachronic" and "synchronic." Because of this it is important to approach a modernist discussion from both perspectives.

When viewing them diachronically, modernist texts should be studied in relation to the current events in the authors' lives and in the world at large. In "Passing the Time: Modernism versus New Criticism," Jeffrey Perl points out that even Eliot, often considered the founder of New Criticism and the great proponent of critics staying within the text and attending to "poetry as poetry," also wanted it known that "any critic seriously concerned with a man's work should be expected to know something about the man's life" (33). With this in mind, this study does not isolate the author's life from a discussion of her fiction but instead integrates her life with her fiction, beginning with her first publication, *Fireweed*, written during the Great Depression, and continuing through *The Orange Tree*, written almost a half century later. Approaching her works in this manner, I evaluate her fiction as it is related to both the public and private events that inspired and affected it. Because modernist fiction is also synchronic, I also address the author's experimentation and development of her fictional style as a result of her private concerns, public interests, and creative inclinations.

In light of the fact that modernism was characterized by words such as "change" and "crisis" and that its authors still sought a common ground and stabilizing force in their work, this study also explores Walker's belief that stability was to be found in language and literature. As such, I offer specific examples of her characters' discussions on writing, literature, and the inconstancy of language. Walker used the metaphor and also seemed to write in the realist tradition. The reconciliation of realism and modernism is discussed further in the chapter "The Aesthetics of Modernism" in light of her use of both metaphoric and metonymic prose.

Chapter one, "The Life and Works of Mildred Walker," offers an overview of this project. Chapter two, "A Working Definition of Modernism," offers readers an overview of modernism both as a term and as a movement. Chapter three, "The Aesthetics of

Modernism," concentrates on the specific aspects of Walker's literary style and experimentation. This chapter also explores her occasionally complex linguistic choices. It is noteworthy that her last works of adult fiction are the most heavily laden with references to literature and mythology, notably *If a Lion Could Talk* and *The Orange Tree*, both of which were produced after her nearly twenty years of teaching English.

In the chapters that follow, I approach modernism from a variety of perspectives: economical, historical, social, and technical. In chapter four, "The Economics of Modernism," the Marxist contention that capitalism flourishes in crisis and constant change is a point of departure for discussion because the characters' tension in many of Walker's novels is created by crises that result from economic change or the competition in a free market economy. Her characters' reactions to these economic forces shed light on her own interpretation of this volatile aspect of modern life. In this discussion I also consider the balance between aesthetic aspiration and economic need that faced modernist writers. Walker's pragmatism is discussed in light of critical essays on Henry James, T. S. Eliot, Ezra Pound, and Ernest Hemingway. Ann Ardis's *New Women, New Novels: Feminism and Early Modernism* and Suzanne Clark's *Sentimental Modernism: Women Writers and the Revolution of the Word* inform the discussion in this chapter. Excerpts from some of the author's final journal entries are also read for her personal feelings before her death.

Chapter five, "Mildred Walker's Wars," follows a chronology of U.S. warfare in the latter part of the nineteenth century and through the twentieth century, as seen through her novels. Particular attention is given to feminist critics' discussions of noncombatants' roles in the discourse of war. Following this analysis I consider the New Woman and the evolution of the American family, surely two of Walker's favorite topics, in chapter 6, "The Mothers of Modernism." Even after the author vowed, "I won't write about the relations between men and women—husbands and wives—again," she could not resist and returned to this subject in her last novel, *The Orange Tree*. She had much to say about women's changing roles in society and the evolving dynamics of the family unit in America from her first novel to her last. Of particular interest in this discussion is how she characterized the relationships between parents and their children—specifically, mothers and daughters. Matthew Bruccoli points out in his study on expatriate modernists that these individuals often depicted themselves and their fictional characters as orphans or, at least, "orphan-like," and his observations inform my argument. Marylu Hill's *Mothering Modernity* as well as feminist discussions in Bonnie Kime Scott's *The Gender of Modernism* and *Refiguring Modernism* are also points of departure for this chapter.

The final chapter, "American Modernists and the Language of Movement," focuses on the effects that rapidly changing technology had on society and its writers. I examine Walker's fictional depictions of both the positive and negative aspects of these rapid changes in her many novels. Beyond the technological changes themselves, the increased movement and displacement of individuals and communities and the phenomenon of "westering" and "eastering" receive attention. This chapter also compares Jackson Benson's comments on Stegner's concept of "eastering" in *Down by the Lemonade Springs* with Walker's own theories.

These chapters can each stand alone. However, I hope that a clearer picture of the ever-evolving term "modernism" and Walker's place in this critical idiom emerges from the collection as a whole. Because no single approach to modernism can stand in isolation, a few of the following chapters cover similar ground. As much as possible, I have avoided repeated interpretations of a single scene; however, multiple interpretations—with varying implications depending upon the critical approach—give further indication of the interdisciplinary nature and concerns of modernist literature.

1. The Life and Work of Mildred Walker

Mildred Walker's prodigious literary career as an author included thirteen published novels and officially began when she was twenty-one, with the publication of an essay entitled "Gargoyles," which she wrote during her senior year at Wells College in New York State. She had enthusiastically entered this private women's college in 1922 under a tuition waiver granted for ministers' daughters, having had ambitions to become a writer since she was nine years old. From Wells College, and after marrying, she continued her education and literary career at the University of Michigan at Ann Arbor, receiving her master's degree in English in 1933, along with the Avery Hopwood Award for her novel *Fireweed*. The success of this novel and its publication that year by Harcourt Brace initiated a partnership that Walker maintained for nearly a half century and eleven more novels, ending with the 1970 publication of *If a Lion Could Talk*. During all these years, Walker maintained her maiden name only for use as a pen name for her fiction. For all other purposes, she referred to herself as Mildred Walker Schemm.

The success of Walker's *Fireweed* helped finance her young family's move from the Midwest to Montana, and the subsequent success of *Winter Wheat* enabled the family to move from their bungalow in Great Falls to their acreage on the banks of the Missouri River. Published in 1944, *Winter Wheat* was her most popular and lucrative novel, but it was by no means her only literary success. In 1939 the Literary Guild of America chose *Dr. Norton's Wife* as their literary selection for January. Her short novel *The Southwest Corner* was transformed in 1954 into a Broadway play and adapted into a Kraft television feature. *The Body of a Young Man* was nominated for the National Book Award in 1960. During these productive years, Walker also regularly wrote book reviews and short stories and clipped reviews of her novels from the pages of the *New York Times Book Review*, the *Saturday Review of Literature*, and the *Book of the Month Club* selections. Although *If a Lion Could Talk* was the last novel by Walker that Harcourt Brace would publish and marked a downturn in her publishing career, the author continued writing for as long as her health permitted. In 1972 Atheneum Press published *A Piece of the World*. Subsequent to this publication, she wrote a novel and a number of short stories and pieces that remained unpublished at her death. By 1992 all of Walker's thirteen novels were out of print, but she lived long enough to see the commencement of their reissue by the University of Nebraska Press, beginning with *Winter Wheat*. This rerelease marked the beginning of a new wave of critical and popular success that the author was able to witness in her final years.

Although Walker was born in Philadelphia, Pennsylvania, she always considered her family's summer residence in Grafton, Vermont, as her childhood home. Both her mother and father had come from this area of Vermont and found themselves in Pennsylvania primarily because of Mildred's father's work as a Baptist minister. However, every summer the family returned to Vermont. In 1916 Mildred's father bought the Grafton house that the family had rented since 1906, which became her home during her retirement and remains in the Schemm family to this day. New England's rich history, landscape, and community influenced six of her published novels: *The Quarry*, *The Southwest Corner*, *The Body of a Young Man*, *If a Lion Could Talk*, *A Piece of the World*, and her last novel, *The Orange Tree*, which features a Vermont setting.

After she had accepted Ferdinand Schemm's marriage proposal in 1927, doing so only after insisting that she could continue her writing career and "not have to do the laundry," she did agree to accompany her husband, a young doctor, to Big Bay on the Upper Peninsula of Michigan. Despite finding herself pregnant and isolated culturally in this remote outpost, Walker was later able, perhaps through the keen senses she had developed as a girl in Vermont and the discipline she had honed in college, to adapt her observations of the natural world and social structure of this small community into her first successful novel, *Fireweed*. Later, when, with some misgivings, she accompanied her young family to Great Falls, Montana, she was again able to harness these same sensibilities to create the rich characterizations, depictions of landscape, and observations of middle-class life featured in *Winter Wheat*, *The Curlew's Cry*, *Unless the Wind Turns*, and *If a Lion Could Talk*. No doubt her keen sense of the natural world, her appreciation of history, and her extraordinary ability to observe and fictionalize the quiet lives and triumphs of ordinary people around her were qualities she had developed in Vermont.

Her careful observations and character studies would find their way into detailed journals she kept for all her writing, often resulting in praise for her novels' detailed depictions of American life. Even today, the 1992 edition of *Winter Wheat* receives accolades for its realistic depictions of Montana and the "real West." Likewise, when *The Brewers' Big Horses* was published in 1940, the beer industry was so impressed by how vividly she had depicted their industry that the *Brewers' Journal* recommended that "every brewery executive, every brewery master and member of the allied trades [read the novel]" (qtd. in Hugo: 89). And when *Dr. Norton's Wife* was published in 1938, it became required reading for nurses because it described so accurately the debilitating effects of multiple sclerosis.

Many of her books have also been touted as good examples of regional writing. However, it is difficult to place her in any one region of the country and label her as a regionalist writer, per se, because for every novel she set in the West there is another set in New England or the Midwest. But if the novels set in a single region are examined apart from her entire literary output, they do fulfill many of the criteria scholars often imply when using the label "regionalist." For instance, in *American Women Regionalists*, Judith Fetterley and Marjorie Pryse distinguish regionalist writers in their specific presentation of the regional experience from within "so as to engage readers' sympathy and identification" (xii), in their characters' development from within their own communities of origin, and in the centrality of landscape to their characters' self-discoveries (xvi). Perhaps because of Walker's ability to invest all her narratives with enough genuine sense of self, and because she writes about landscapes that she personally inhabited and studied, her readers seldom sense that her stories are from an outsider's perspective and so easily label her work as regionalist.

Despite the variety of geographic settings and broad subject matter in her novels, this label of "regional writer" persists. Especially today, Walker is most often referred to as a Montana writer. There are a number of explanations for this label. First, although only four of her novels are set in Montana, she wrote nine of her novels while residing in the state between 1933 and 1955. Second, she is best known, particularly today, for a novel set in Montana, *Winter Wheat*. This novel is considered by some to be the first quintessentially female *bildungsroman* about the modern western woman. Ann Ronald, in her essay "Montana Maturity," discusses *Winter Wheat* as such, claiming that it "finally relies on the earth itself to explain fully the germination and maturation of its female hero" (105). Third, her family's presence in the state and dedication to the Montana literary scene has had much to do with the resurgence of popularity and critical acclaim her novels began to receive in the 1990s. Walker is one of four family members with pieces in *The Last Best Place*, a popular anthology of Montana writers. The book features excerpts from Walker's fiction and samples of poems from her son-in-law, Richard Hugo, her daughter, Ripley Hugo, and her grandson, Matthew Hansen. Certainly, no other single family has a stronger presence in this collection of writings about Montana. Furthermore, longtime Montana resident Ripley Hugo has continuously promoted her mother's works by attending readings and conferences and by recently producing her mother's biography, *Writing for Her Life: The Novelist Mildred Walker*. Notably, *Winter Wheat* was the "One Book Montana" selection for 2003 in conjunction with Montana's fourth annual state book festival. However, "regional writer" is not a label Walker would have chosen for herself. After reading a 1950 *Kirkus Review* that praised her as a "regional novelist," she lamented that such terms would automatically limit her readership (Hugo 194).

Walker had reacted similarly when Joe Howard, family friend and author of *Montana: High, Wide, and Handsome*, tried to dismiss her works, claiming he did not read women's romances. Ripley Hugo also chronicles the fact that her mother became sullen whenever book reviews characterized her fiction as being "warm," "homey," or "sentimental" (Hugo 135). But there are valid reasons why readers might have sought these labels as well. Relationships between men and women play a role in the plots of all her novels. For a public that focuses primarily on these relationships when reading her novels, such labels might seem apt. Likewise, most of her novels, though not all, feature strong-willed and ambitious female protagonists. Often, their struggle for independence is central to the novels. For this reason, a number of modern scholars have suggested offering feminist readings of her works. For instance, in Mary Swander's introduction to the 1995 edition of *Light from Arcturus*, she indicated that the novel represented the concerns of "current feminism" in that it portrayed "a perspective of 'trailing spouses' [. . .] socialized to give up self in the service of community and family" (x). However, when Mildred Walker read the introduction, she disagreed completely with Swander's assessment, once again resisting any attempts to label her works.

A possible explanation for her resistance to any labels, particularly feminism, may be found in the words of a friend of the Schemm's, Sharon Bryan. In her introduction to *Where We Stand: Women Poets on Literary Tradition*, Bryan offers the following: "Some feminist rhetoric seems to reduce complex issues to a matter of choosing sides, and [. . .] I think many women poets [and writers] have been reluctant to voice their concerns because they were afraid of being misunderstood, labeled, pigeonholed, dismissed" (Introduction vii–xiii).

Given that some critical labels and approaches limit interpretations of the author's works and that she herself was resistant to labels, reading Walker's novels as modernist texts seems an agreeable and apt approach. With a career that spanned the best part of the twentieth century, a marked interest and concern for a rapidly changing society, and a propensity for experimentation in both style and subject matter, Walker employs themes and styles that are captured in modernism. During her long career, she was able to take part in the exciting development of the novel predicted by writers she admired greatly—Henry James, E. M. Forster, and Virginia Woolf, who themselves fostered stylistic adaptations by altering points of view and time sequences and by using unreliable narrators. Psychological realism and the implementation of metaphors and other devices of literary compression all had the consequence of forcing readers to become more participatory in the interpretation and subsequent appreciation of modernist fiction. Not only was Walker aware of these changes, she took advantage of the broadening of possibilities for her novels' characters and subject matter, offering fiction that featured narratives told through the viewpoint of disabled, psychologically troubled, and aged protagonists.

Although readers might find little evidence in the author's earlier novels of the stylistic modernism that characterized some aspects of her later works, her social and thematic concerns were modernist from her first publications. For instance, though *Fireweed* follows a traditional chronological sequence and is told from one narrative perspective, it is rife with the observations and concerns of many modernist writers. If readers study the opening pages of *Fireweed* they will discover a vivid description and commentary on the over-harvested and denuded forests of Northern Michigan. Even in her first published novel, Walker was concerned by the effects of commercialization, not only on the landscape, but on the attitudes and ambitions of people in the most remote spots of North America.

With a cinematographer's eye, the novelist introduces young Celie Henderson in *Fireweed* with the image of her high-heeled opera pumps, carefully navigating the mud and cracks on the broken boardwalks of Flat Point, in marked contrast to the other heavy feet tramping along in gold-seal boots. Although this seventeen-year-old girl has never seen life beyond the Upper Peninsula, her head is full of dreams. Cinema has come to Flat Point. She twists her hair like Greta Garbo. She saves her money from working at the company store to buy pretty dresses from mail-order catalogs. She is, in fact, discontent, sensing that the world is on the move and that she is missing out. This discontent creates the initial tension in the novel. However, Walker inserts greater concerns than the dreams of this small town girl in the conflicts between the wealthy mill owners and the laborers as well as those caused by the pecking order in the community's complex ethnic mix. Then, the Great Depression hits and closes mines and mills. Like other towns struck by economic hardship, Flat Point is abandoned. The novel's characters make their exodus to the urban centers, but Celie's young family does not. Initially, she is disappointed not to leave, but eventually she comes to accept that personal independence is worth more than material possessions. Despite this ending, the narrator reminds her readers that the world is on the move and that Celie accepts her life in Flat Point only with the knowledge that her children will not.

Many of the issues in Walker's first novel reemerge in subsequent works. In *Winter Wheat*, for example, Ellen cannot return to college because the family's wheat crop is unprofitable due to a poor growing season and prewar commodity prices. In *The Curlew's Cry*, Pamela Lacey tries to reinvent the family's western enterprise by transforming a bankrupt cattle ranch into a dude operation. This novel also fictionalizes the union action of the region's mine workers in response to the indifference of their corporate owners and the tensions caused by the tightening grip eastern owners exert on western lands. The plots in *The Quarry*, *Light from Arcturus*, and *The Brewers' Big Horses* are also driven by the author's understanding of the rapid changes in the U.S. economy that threaten to destroy many families' businesses and ways of life. Even *The Southwest Corner* can be read as a reaction to the social effects of the economic upheavals in American society. When the novel's elderly protagonist, Marcia Elder, finds that she can no longer live alone, she studies her New England home and remembers that there was a time when extended families lived together and the southwest corner of the house was a separately deeded parcel, allowing the elderly members of the family to live their last days in dignity and privacy that this era has passed over. Now, the rural population of New England has moved off to more prosperous areas. Despite the fact that families and communities have been scattered in search of economic opportunity, however, Marcia Elder remains in Vermont and eventually finds a way to create her own social security and maintain the custodianship over the land that has sustained her family for generations.

Not only was Walker aware of changes in the economic system, she was also cognizant of alterations in men's and women's roles and of the family structure in general as the twentieth century progressed. A number of her protagonists are working women, battling and sometimes overcoming stereotypes and other obstacles in a man's world. Some are also women who deeply question their traditional roles as mothers, wives, and members of a community. Several novels feature divorcées, while even *Winter Wheat*, published in 1944, offers in its conclusion the possibility of a new form of nuclear family when its protagonist befriends an older war veteran and his young child.

Walker was also interested in the rapidly changing ethnic composition of American society and its associated tensions. *Winter Wheat* captures metaphorically the evolving face of the American middle class. The winter wheat crop is a hybrid of grain that is strong enough to grow in the dry high plains of eastern Montana. It is a cross, as Ellen is, between gene pools from America and Russia. The tension that Ellen feels in her own household stemming from the differences between her New England father and Russian immigrant mother are tantamount to the young woman's confusion about love and mutual understanding. Even to Ellen, her Russian mother is often foreign. Throughout the novel the question begs itself: if a daughter can feel alienated from her own mother, what must others feel toward a foreigner? And why has Ellen assimilated so little of her mother's rich cultural heritage? There are no easy answers to these questions. In one particularly poignant scene, Ellen's family drives to town for Easter services. Somehow, when they arrive, Ellen's mother assumes that they will attend her church and her father assumes they will attend his. When Ellen's mother offers to solve the dilemma by remaining in the car, Ellen's father refuses her offer, and the family does not attend any Easter service but simply returns home in silence. The emptiness and sadness of this particular scene capture much of the conflict in the novel. It also displays a modernist ambivalence about the role of religion in this new, complex, and increasingly secularized world.

The novelist returns to this question many times in her work, particularly in *If a Lion Could Talk*. This historical novel fictionalizes the failures of a young missionary among the Blackfeet Indians. Not only is Mark Ryegate unable to convert the Blackfeet to Christianity, he even fails to communicate with them and begins to question the church's right to try and exert a presence in an environment where he finds himself so completely ignorant. With his confidence and faith shaken, he returns to his church in New England. Upon returning, with eyes open, he realizes the absurdity in thinking that he could ever truly communicate with anyone. While Mark struggles to communicate with his congregation, his own wife has been unsuccessfully trying to communicate with him. These characters' efforts to reach out and share with each other echo the modernist concern with trying to find meaning in a world where it no longer seems to exist. At the novel's conclusion, Mark Ryegate's wife, Harriet, wisely observes: "But was communicating with a person really that important? [. . .] How stupid she had been, insisting that they must talk everything out, always say what they meant, when they themselves couldn't always have known [. . .]" (265).

Throughout both her writing life and her career as an English professor—she was an associate professor of English at Wells College, teaching there between 1955 and 1968, and also taught for several summers at the Bread Loaf Writers' Conference, at Castleton College in Vermont, and as a Fulbright professor in Japan in 1960—Mildred Walker attempted to find meaning and personal satisfaction in words and literature. Her novels are rich with references to other books and questions about the meanings of words, as are her journals and notes for her lectures. Even in her last novel, *The Orange Tree*, the author has Olive question the true meaning of the word "joy." This young woman asks herself what the word truly signifies when it can be used in the names of a dish detergent and a cookbook. The novel's other protagonist, Tiresa, a dying English professor, makes sense of her world by reading Keats, Chekhov, and other authors and by spending her last days trying to write—similar to the author herself. It is no coincidence that Ripley Hugo titled her mother's biography *Writing for Her Life*.

Perhaps Walker captured her own feelings on the importance of the written word best when, in her later years, she discussed her father with her daughter. She told Ripley that her father was the biggest influence on her writing and that, as a young girl, with pen in hand, she had sat on the floor of his office while he wrote his weekly sermons and had imitated him. She explained to her daughter how important her father's belief in his own eloquence had been, saying, "Why, he was convinced that he could bring any man to see reason [with his words]" (qtd. in Hugo: 218). Mildred Walker wrote with the very same conviction.

2. A Working Definition of Modernism

In recent years both the traditional modernist canon and scholars' understandings of the term "modernism" have undergone radical rehabilitation in light of postmodernism and cultural studies. As a proponent of this rehabilitation and redefinition, Stella Deen writes that "when literature is no longer viewed as an enclave in isolation either from history or the institutions and discourses of its time, new and meaningful portions of the cultural dialogue in which it is engaged can be heard" (6). This "enclave in isolation" has often been described in terms of the traditional division between high and low culture, a bifurcation of American literature often attributed to the influence of high modernism. However, postmodernism's recent and continued interest in neglected and forgotten twentieth-century literature, expanded by the increasingly interdisciplinary nature of literary studies, has led to the formation of new scholarly journals and organizations. Notable additions include the *International Review of Modernism*, founded in 1997; the *Modernist Studies Association*, formed in 1999; and the recently initiated *Space Between Society*, dedicated to a study of the often neglected literature written between the two world wars. These organizations and many individual scholars continue to challenge the previously limited canon and definition of modernism.

For instance, Matthew Bruccoli suggests a new approach to defining modernism by focusing upon two components and criteria often used to discuss literary accomplishments. These criteria are modernist works' synchronic appeal and their diachronic import. By "synchronic," Bruccoli refers to the text's ability to remain meaningful despite its having been written some time ago: a "picture of the whole." "Diachronic" refers to what the writing can teach its audience about the specific historical and social contexts in which it was written with the details of its particular era revealed. Although "universal" and "particular" might seem less technical ways to describe these criteria, Bruccoli points out that "universal [. . .] assumes that certain values and beliefs are ingrained in the human condition regardless of time and place—an assumption that soon proves impossible to substantiate" (60). Synchronic relevance, instead, implies that readers can relate a piece of writing to other times—that is, rather than saying that a piece expresses a "timeless truth," they can relate to its characters, themes, and concerns and find a pertinence in their own lives.

Many of the interests, tendencies, and qualities often attributed to modernists can also be found in the works of writers living in other historical periods. However, in "The Language of Modernist Fiction," David Lodge argues that modernists have "a family resemblance" in terms of literary style, or what Roland Barthes calls "écriture"—a "mode of writing" (qtd. in Bradbury: 482). Lodge further suggests that this family resemblance is either implicit or explicit and that modernist authors' aesthetic reactions were primarily driven by thoughtful philosophical and intellectual inquiries and beliefs resulting from their own life experiences and personal engagement with the issues of their day.

Peter Childs's text *Modernism* focuses on a redefinition of modernism. He approaches this project by summarizing the many ways in which the term has been interpreted and the period distinguished from others. He also suggests that perhaps the easiest way to define modernism is by "the idea that identity exists through difference" and that modernism is not realism or postmodernism (2). Childs offers his own definition of modernism in the following:

> Modernism is associated with attempts to render human subjectivity in ways more real than realism: to represent consciousness, perception, emotion, meaning and the individual's relation to society through interior monologue, stream of consciousness, tunneling, defamiliarisation, rhythm, irresolution and other terms to be described later [. . .]. Modernist writers therefore struggled, in Ezra Pound's phrase, to 'make it new', to modify if not overturn existing modes of representation, partly by pushing them towards the abstract or the introspective, and to express the new sensibilities of their times: in a compressed, condensed, complex literature of the city, of industry and technology, wars, machinery and speed, mass markets and communication, of internationalism, the New Woman, the aesthete, the nihilist and the *flaneur*. (3–4)

Supplementing Childs's definition, in his introduction to *The Future of Modernism*, Hugh Witemeyer adds that modernism may be characterized as:

> (1) a revulsion against urban, industrial, bourgeois society, with its technologies of mass warfare; (2) a disposition to interpret modern experiences in terms of patterns derived from archaic cultures and ancient mythologies; (3) a fascination with the unconscious and irrational activities of the human psyche; and (4) a rejection of Post-Renaissance techniques of naturalistic representation in favor of spare, elemental, disjunctive, and ironic modes. (ix)

After offering this definition, however, Witemeyer, unlike Childs, argues that modernism's definition has changed with the effects of postmodern thought. No longer should postmodernism and modernism be defined by "simplistic binary oppositions," nor should they necessarily be viewed as existing on a continuum where one naturally leads to the next. Instead, postmodernism should be credited with "decoupling modernism from formalism and New Criticism," thus offering a "rereading of modernism from a postmodern perspective" (3). Similarly, other contributors to *The Future of Modernism* in fact implement postmodern theory to explain modernism. In "The Postmodernity of Modernism," Sanford Schwartz expands on Witemeyer's comments by suggesting that current critical revisionist work on modernism should aim "neither to dissolve nor to defend the distinction between modernism and postmodernism, but rather, to understand the difference that the latter has had on the former" (10). Schwartz argues that, to a certain extent, a text can be modern or postmodern, depending upon how we read it and what we read. He suggests that the traditional split between modernism and postmodernism might be viewed as "modernism cut in half"—and that what we call postmodernism "is nothing other than the forgotten side of modernism" (16). Hence, the marked effort we have witnessed in recent postmodern years to produce new critical editions of previously out-of-print texts, such as those by Walker.

Schwartz points out that the traditional placement of texts and authors on a continuum from naturalism, through realism and modernism, to postmodernism also influences who reads a text and how it is read. In fact, it could be argued that a single reader might interpret a given text as both a work of realism and modernism. Furthermore, if that same reader studies a writer's oeuvre on its own continuum, the writing might appear more realist earlier in the career and more modernist at a later date.

Certainly this concept of authorial change in style and subject matter must be addressed in a discussion of an author's oeuvre. For instance, Walker wrote for over sixty years and lived through almost the entirety of the twentieth century. Her work altered in style and subject matter during these years, which is characteristic of the work of many modernist authors, and her novels, despite her modernist sensibilities, are most often praised for their realism. This use of the term "realism" is confusing and potentially misleading. Although Walker's fiction is presented in seemingly realist terms, readers should note that she never uses an omniscient narrator and often deliberately creates empty spaces, utilizes literary compression, and relies upon the reader to fill in the gaps and draw meanings from these literary devices.

Jo Ann Middleton, who studied Willa Cather's use of these same techniques in her detailed study *Willa Cather's Modernism*, argues that Cather's use of vacuoles (deliberate gaps in the text that force a reader to question reality) and her assumption that she is sometimes writing for a "fine reader" are two qualities that distinguish Cather (and other writers) as a modernist. Cather herself defined a "fine reader" as "the person with quickness and richness of mentality, fineness of spirituality [. . .]. It's the shape of the head that's of importance, the something in it that can bring an ardor and honesty to a masterpiece and make it all over until it becomes a personal possession" (qtd. in Middleton: 67). There is evidence in Walker's style that she concurred with Cather about how readers interact with the text.

Modernism's ideologies were often bound up in a reverence for literature and the written word. Walker, like many other modernist authors, invariably has a subtext in her novels. Most frequently the subtext concerns the writer paying deference to literature and to the concerns of other writers, both living and dead. Repeatedly, her characters read, write, and discuss literature, which, in turn, enhances the theme she is developing in her own stories. Often, her characters are writing about writing, mirroring her own efforts.

Although Walker questions the past and the verity of memories and history, she never turns from or disregards the historic or literary past as a point of reference for her characters and her fiction. Her fiction helps substantiate Childs's claim that modernism has both an historical and an ideological orientation.

In Childs's definition, modernism is literature of the city, of industry and technology, war, machinery and speed, mass markets and communication, of internationalism, the New

Woman, the aesthete, the nihilist and the *flaneur*. But this is not a complete definition. Childs fails to mention the rural, the traditional, the optimistic, or the recently liberated, with the exception of the New Woman. It can certainly be argued that modernism was "of the country" as well as "of the city" and that the effects of modern life reverberated as strongly on the family farm as they did in the urban centers. In fact, one cannot discuss modernism relative to the city and industrialization without considering the depopulation of many rural areas. Similarly, Roy Harvey Pearce, in *The Continuity of American Poetry*, argues that Robert Frost's "rural poetry" was really very much a reaction to urbanization and modernity, "a momentary stay against confusion," that "Frost was driven to mountain and farm, to wholeness 'beyond confusion,' to life simplified" (275), and that his poetry should not be seen as escapist but very much engaged with modern life. At the turn of the century, over fifty percent of the U.S. population lived on farms. By the 1990s less than 2 percent of the population lived on farms. A similar depopulation and collapse of communities also occurred in non-farming, rural areas, where lumber and other trades had traditionally supported a population. Walker's novels focused on rural life, but in doing so they were still reacting to modernity. Furthermore, her characters usually were not aesthetes, nihilists, or *flaneurs*. More often than not, they were working people with mixed feelings about both the future and the past. She presents both the positive and negative effects of technological, economic, and social change.

Walker's approach to these changes can often be characterized as ambivalent, and it might be conjectured that if she felt strongly about an issue, she often withheld her own position from her fiction. James McFarlane, in "The Mind of Modernism," pinpoints this characteristic ambiguity on the part of modernists and suggests that they had "a natural reluctance [. . .] to say 'in simple words' what it was they were at" (88). McFarlane further explains that the modernist purpose might be viewed as a resolution between Hegel and Kierkegaard (Hegel's "both/and" versus Kierkegaard's "either/or") and suggests that the "Modernist formula is 'both/and' and 'or either/or'" (88). Walker was not only aware of these theories but actively studied them. In her personal journals, she quotes Kierkegaard quite regularly, and it is evident that she studied him while she worked on her last novel, *The Orange Tree*, and that his philosophical stance was something she incorporated into both her characters' thoughts as well as the basic themes of her novels. Examples of modernist ambiguity are apparent in her earliest novels, which concern the struggles and depopulation of the rural American countryside and depict how families adapted to changing times. Her own natural reluctance to voice her opinion about these changes is apparent in her first novel, *Fireweed*. When the big city owners close their lumber mills in northern Michigan because of the Great Depression, Walker does not stop, as some writers might have, with the perspective that the owners only saw the workers as adjuncts to their industry and never cared about the people, communities, and the natural world their dehumanizing organizations destroyed in their wake. Instead, she carefully studies the choices these workers faced after the mill-owners left. Some workers move south to work in Michigan's growing industrial belt. Walker, however, does not have her main protagonists move. Instead, they discover a means to create their own business selling Christmas trees, firewood, fish, and wreaths. *Fireweed*'s quiet ending is realistic and believable; such a survival would have been a plausible economic possibility for this family. Here, the author reminds her readers that although the Great Depression can be viewed as a social and economic disaster, it can also be seen as having flushed out some of the inefficient and dehumanizing aspects of an earlier version of American capitalism and as having precipitated many positive changes, some of which allowed families and smaller enterprises an entrepreneurial entry into the U.S. marketplace that had previously been denied them. *Fireweed*'s ending exposes both the dead end of many mill-workers' lives as they are pulled into the industrial build-up of the Midwest and, at the same time, demonstrates the new possibilities for those who sought an alternate path.

Walker returns many times in her fiction to the ambiguity of interpreting modern life and to the subject of American families adjusting their expectations and activities to account for the rapid changes brought about by technological developments. Certainly, she did not have any blind-eyed optimism about the future; instead, in her own careful and studied way, she explored small opportunities for her characters that allowed them to survive and maintain their dignity. Her work is not pessimistic. Because of this, she is different from many well-known modernist writers. In fact, in viewing modernity as a mixed blessing, offering both new opportunities but also new forms of ensnarement, Walker's perspective is similar to that of many minority writers. Alice Gambrell, in *Women Intellectuals, Modernism, and Difference: Transatlantic Culture 1919–1945*, recognizes this same awareness of both modernism's new-found opportunities and its challenges to individuals who were part of these modern social upheavals in the work of Zora Neale Hurston, Ella Deloria, Leonora Carrington, H. D. (Hilda Doolittle), and Frida Kahlo.

On this note, Childs's definition and focus on the fact that modernism was not only a "literature of change, but a literature of crisis" (14) need to be reevaluated. Although modernity was marked by change, crisis carries a pessimistic connotation. Childs indicates that most modernist writers viewed the "crisis" that occurred in modern times as primarily dehumanizing and negative. Although he later admits that modernism has often been characterized as largely Eurocentric and a reaction to mass culture and feminization settling upon a masculine elitism, he characterizes modernists as disenfranchised and disillusioned and, in doing so, indicates his own bias, similar to those critics with a pre-postmodern notion of modernism (22). Perhaps because of this bias he overlooks those members of society whose groups had been disenfranchised and disillusioned for many years before the modernist revolution. He fails to mention those who hardly noticed the arrival of the Great Depression because they had always been poor. Certainly, for many members of an elite and largely patriarchal society, the changes in the twentieth century shook, if not destroyed, their way of life and may well have resulted in their disillusionment and feelings of disenfranchisement. But while the rise of the middle class, conspicuous consumption, and other aspects of mass culture may have eroded the position previously held by the aristocracy and many members of the middle class, including artists and writers, the changes also created opportunities for other groups and voices that had never been heard before. For these people modernity was an improvement over previous times, and their literature testifies to the opportunities it provided.

Walker's ambivalence indicates that she viewed modernity in both lights. Although she certainly didn't come from a privileged background, her family was middle class and had been landowners in the United States for centuries. Moreover, the changes in the U.S. economy caused her family a number of crises, both destroying and creating opportunities. Additionally, because she moved a number of times and lived for many years in rural New England, the Midwest, and Montana, and was a careful observer of the people around her, she was constantly reminded and aware of how the changes in the U.S. economy had altered various ways of life. At the same time, however, because she was trained as a writer to remain somewhat detached from her subject matter, she was also able to fictionalize different outcomes of these changes for middle-class Americans. For instance, in *The Curlew's Cry*, she was able to create readerly sympathy for the novel's family-owned ranches that could no longer compete with eastern conglomerates and, at the same time, also celebrate those who were able to adapt, survive, and sometimes even prosper. In *The Curlew's Cry* it is the family's daughter who transforms its bankrupt cattle ranch into a thriving guest ranch. The destruction of the patriarchal cattle ranch leaves a void that a single, ambitious woman is able to fill, creating an opportunity that had not previously existed. Similarly, in her historical novel *The Quarry*, Walker offers both a sympathetic portrayal of the demise of the family's quarry business, wrought by both the Civil War and its resulting technological advances in concrete production, and, simultaneously, a celebration of the success of an emancipated slave, who moves into an old farm next to the quarry and builds a life and family around his own piece of land and his recently freed wife. Again, *Winter Wheat*'s fictional depiction of both the physical and emotional injuries sustained by the young protagonist's father in World War I and the neighborhood debates over U.S. entry into World War II indicate the author's personal repulsion toward the horrors of war and the zeal of young farm boys who eagerly sought the battlefront. However, this initial repulsion on the part of the narrator concerning the war is complicated later in the text by the inclusion of comments made by the protagonist's Russian-immigrant mother when she shares her more positive memories of the effects of World War I with her daughter. In these, she recalls some of the nightmares of her life in war-torn Russia and the subsequent peace that she found in the American West as a result of her marriage to a U.S. soldier stationed in her village. Here again, a reader senses the author's ambivalence about the issues surrounding U.S. participation in the war. As a modernist writer, Walker walked a middle road in much of her fiction, presenting neither a wholly optimistic nor pessimistic viewpoint but instead consistently creating a text sympathetic to the struggles of individual human beings, always in an attempt to write realistically while also portraying and reacting to the many changes in modern life.

In his definition of modernism Childs also notes that modernist literature was reacting to technological change, speed, and the New Women. These aspects of modern life appear throughout Walker's fiction. For instance, many of her texts feature female protagonists who struggle for and achieve individual agency in both their private and public lives. Furthermore, her fictional depictions of the evolution of New Women are inextricably tied to technological change and the speed of modernity. In *Light from Arcturus*, a young Julia Hauser attends the Philadelphia Exposition of 1876 on her honeymoon. Her impressions from this experience lay the foundation for the tension in her life. After the visit to the exposition, now aware of the great changes occurring in the world outside her small town, Julia is discontent living with a mercantilist in a safe and traditional Midwest town. When she attends the Chicago World's Fair in 1893 and is again reminded of advancements in technology and the speed of modern life in the city, Julia decides that she will not allow her life or those of her children to continue in a rural American backwater. The steps that she then takes to be part of the exciting, fast-paced world move her even further into the realm of the New Women. Again, in *The Brewers' Big Horses*, the novelist portrays an American family embroiled in both the technological and social changes of the turn of the century. As a young widow, Sara Bolster decides to literally take the reins of the family brewery after her husband dies from an accident with the brewery's Clydesdales. Ironically, although her family is supportive of the suffragette movement, they consider it inappropriate for a young woman like Sara to even attempt to run a brewery. Amidst this family struggle, Sara is further confronted by the technological and social developments that threaten the brewery's existence as well as the family's finances and way of life. Caught between Prohibition and new forms of mass production and marketing within the beer industry, Julia Hauser modernizes the family brewery and ultimately creates an even greater success than her predecessors, developing a business that is a model of modern industry and marketing developments. However, once again, Walker does not end her novel with the triumphs of modern life. Throughout the text, she sympathetically portrays the loneliness and sacrifices her protagonist must make in her personal life in order to sustain the business and to fulfill her own entrepreneurial ambitions. *The Brewers' Big Horses* reminds readers of both the grace and tradition of an earlier America that are lost in the modern world through the metaphor of the work horses. Walker accomplishes this without any invocations of sentimentalism over the past; the narrator reminds her readers that it was the same beautiful horses Sara loved as a little girl that sped because of a sudden noise and caused her husband's death. Many of the issues Walker explores in this novel are similar to those considered by Henry Adams in "The Virgin and the Dynamo" from *The Education of Henry Adams*, in which he expresses both a fascination for what he witnesses at the Paris Exposition and grave misgivings for the future of society in this new technological world.

Critics and historians alike have identified the influences of Marx, Darwin, Freud, Saussure, Einstein, and Nietzsche as being key to understanding many of these changes as well as modernity itself. For example, in discussing these essential figures of history and change, Childs suggests several natural and logical categories in which to approach the relationship between these historical figures and modernism. Marx, he explains, emphasized the polarities of modern life through economic and social theory. Marx characterized these polarities as individual versus communal efforts for the betterment of society at large. He highlighted the alienating effects of capitalism, its inevitable industrialization, its creation of insatiable desires and drives, and the nature of crisis endemic to a free market economy. Childs paraphrases Marx's criticism of capitalism by adding that because of "the flattening of status introduced by the authority of an exchange-value society, many of the distinctions afforded previous societies were stripped away. A market economy recognized no privileges in its commodity-based and competitive world. Consequently, artists were stripped of their status in society. Reacting against this, they created a new importance, attempting to put aesthetics above all else" (30). In this, a possible explanation for the bifurcation of literature into what is often referred to as "highbrow" and "lowbrow" emerges. Moreover, Marx describes the dynamics of capitalism as a process of constant creation, destruction, and recreation. Modernists often present a picture of the world in a similar light.

From Charles Darwin, the concepts of natural selection and evolution contributed to a modern sense that the struggle for self-preservation and promotion emerge as essential components of life. The belief in evolution and natural selection inherently meant progress undermined the traditional beliefs in God and organized religion. The individual and group struggles and the unavoidable conflict resulting from this process of natural selection are topics that found their way into many modernist texts, particularly those that focused on war. The increasing secularization resulting from society's acceptance of Darwin's theories is also a theme of many modernist works.

Additionally, Sigmund Freud, father of psychoanalysis, encouraged the study and value of the subconscious, and the inner workings of the individual mind are paramount to his studies. Although the concept that a fixed picture of reality was as varied as the individuals who perceived it was in many ways liberating, Childs points out that "with such an emphasis on the individual, it also brought with it feelings of alienation and angst after centuries of the certainties of shared religion" (46). Freud's interest in memory and dreams and in the distinction between chronological and psychological time were also integral aspects of modernist studies, both stylistically and thematically. For example, in *Refiguring Modernism: The Women of 1928*, Bonnie Kime Scott argues that the tradition of psychological realism is an integral aspect of feminist modernism (236). She offers the example of modernist writer Virginia Woolf, who captured the complexity of time in her novel, *Mrs. Dalloway*. In this novel, a few chronological seconds last pages. For another example of modernists' complex perspectives on time, Childs points out that Proust, popular amongst modernists, is often quoted for his statement, "Reality takes shape in memory alone" (50). Freud's influence can also be found in many modernist texts that integrate memory and varying points of view into fictional presentations, which force readers to question the narratives' presentations of reality and truth. In Childs's discussion of Freud, he writes that "[w]ith the advent of psychoanalysis, among other new ideas, the theological search for God had been replaced by the epistemological quest for self-knowledge; enlightenment was not to be found in Christianity or in society, but in the self, in the individual subjective subconscious" (54).

One of the hallmarks of modernist writing is its attentiveness to memory and self-referentiality. Modernist writers frequently depict their personal experiences, albeit often in altered or enhanced forms. While other writers have drawn on personal experience, the practice is especially common with many modernist writers. Not coincidentally, the personal and public lives of modernism's key figures have also been of interest to modernist critics and readers, even those who claimed to be New Critics. Perhaps because modernists questioned the reliability of both language and shared beliefs as a point for common reference but still sought a shared fulcrum between themselves and their readers, they often utilized self-reference as this fulcrum in both their fiction and promotional materials. The life, work, and critical reception of Ernest Hemingway, for example, are often inextricably bound. His fiction seemed to demand that he live some version of each event he captured in his writing. This phenomenon early in his life could have been the result of his journalistic training; however, as his career progressed and he continued to seek out events specifically for his fiction, it is apparent that the deep connection between his life and work was complex and more than a side effect of journalistic training. This cross-over between life and literature is also apparent in the life and work of John Steinbeck. Prior to writing *Grapes of Wrath*, Steinbeck went out and helped his friend, Tom Collins, promote, build, and manage the demonstration camps for the victims of the Dust Bowl in California. Steinbeck was personally involved in this relief effort, witnessing the horrors of the crowded camps for several years before he began writing his famous novel.

Childs also points out that Saussure's theories on language were both liberating and alienating to members of the modern public and were therefore anxiety-producing. Language could no longer be relied upon for either accuracy or veracity. Saussure asserted that man was a product of his language, with all its associated cultural predilections and inherent prejudices. Modernists continued to assert their belief that language remained the fulcrum to a shared world, even as they anxiously perceived the complexities inherent in this tool and frequently questioned its accuracy and import. These anxieties, in fact, often form the tension in their fiction and poetry. There are numerous examples of modernists' anxieties about language and their attempts to preserve its integrity through new and creative means. Certainly the most famous declaration of this struggle is found in the words of Ezra Pound, who asserted that artists should "make it new" while "standing on the shoulders of giants." Pound expressed his and many other modernists' continued belief in language and literature while also admitting his reservations and concerns that poets and other artists were caught in a cheap, deceptive, and imprisoning rubric.

Friedrich Wilhelm Nietzsche also contributed to the self-scrutinizing and aesthetic concerns that would characterize the work of many modernists. Childs points out that Nietzsche's assault on organized religion and opposition to "the mindless masses" were frequent sources of modernist concern. Furthermore, Nietzsche's argument that people of the modern age had lost contact with tragic myth, especially the Dionysian principle of dream and chaos, encouraged a number of modernists to turn away from scientific rationalism to myths. One study of this phenomenon appears in Franz Kuna's essay "The Janus-faced Novel: Conrad, Musil, Kafka, Mann," which offers an example of Nietzsche's influence on modernists through Kuna's examination of what Nietzsche referred to as "the Janus face of modern man." In this concept, man is both "destructively creative" (forming the temporal world of individuation and becoming, a process destructive of unity) and "creatively destructive" (devouring the illusory universe of individuation, a process involving the recreation of unity), which all contributes to man's duplicitous actions that vacillate between egoism and altruism, absolute idealism and absolute barbarism (445). Kanus recognizes the appeal that the dialectic between form and formlessness, optimism and tragic pessimism held for modern man. A number of modernist writers explored Nietzsche's belief that below the surface of this well-ordered modern life, primitive and anarchistic forces festered. Franz Kuna offers Conrad's *Heart of Darkness* as one such example. Perhaps not coincidentally, Mildred Walker had Conrad's novel in mind (evidenced in her journal entries) when she wrote *If a Lion Could Talk*, about a nineteenth-century missionary's trip up the Missouri.

Although Walker's earlier novels display an ambiguity in their philosophical positions, her later works, particularly those written after her husband's death, offer more evidence of this Nietzschean influence. For instance, in her last two novels she explores the complex, dark, and duplicitous nature of man. In *If a Lion Could Talk*, the young minister, who thinks he only wants to do good in the world, must inevitably face the fact that part of his own enthusiastic and seemingly altruistic goals has been fed by his own egoism. And in *The Orange Tree*, Walker examines the complex dynamics of the relationship between a husband and wife. The marriage and its subsequent unity create a sense of wholeness for each of the partners, but the novel also captures a dark and lingering concern in the far reaches of each partner's mind, that their love and interdependence is, or will become, their hell. In fact, the last words Tiresa speaks before she dies make reference to her husband in what initially can be interpreted as a "happy time" when, years earlier, they wandered through a Greco-Roman amphitheater where Paulo had jumped on the empty stage and pretended to act. But, as she dies, Tiresa whispers, "He was Prometheus" (290).

Many scholarly discussions of modernists' search for a common and shared reality omit a discussion of "place." However, place is arguably one of the most common points of reference and stabilizing elements in the fiction of many modernist writers and should be included both in a discussion of modernism and in an explanation of these writers' search for stability and points of common reference for their readers. In *As I Lay Dying*, William Faulkner makes it clear to his readers that reality and truth are as varied and unreliable as his narrators. There is, however, one fixed point of reference in Faulkner's work, and it is a place: Yoknapatawpha County, Mississippi. Again, in "Big Two-Hearted River," Hemingway secures his meaning and shares his reality with the reader through his vivid descriptions of northern Michigan and of a river that has not changed. Painstakingly, he has a war-weary Nick Adams travel through the burnt-out, lumbered landscape of the Upper Peninsula, utilizing the landscape as a metaphor for the current emotional terrain of Nick Adams. It is only when Nick returns to the river and deliberately re-creates each motion, from memory, of the boy he once was, that he finds any meaning. Certainly, American writers' reverence of place and use of it as a secure point of reference began long before Hemingway. Another example of the use of place can be found in Steinbeck's *The Red Pony*. Steinbeck has Jody return repeatedly to the water trough as a point of reference when his world is too confusing or hurtful. Similarly, Virginia Woolf uses London as the only secure point of reference in *Mrs. Dalloway*. In this novel Woolf experiments with traditional notions of time and with perceptions, but her inclusion of Big Ben and the streets of London serve as a stabilizing image and assist in guiding both her characters and readers through an otherwise foggy and unknown terrain. Undoubtedly, place is a point of stability in many modernist texts, and Walker's use of it is integral to her fiction as well as to her characters' growth and security. Elaine Jahner's recent critical study, *Spaces of the Mind*, characterizes place as not only a stabilizing force for Walker's characters in *Winter Wheat* but also as the genesis of meaningful and shared discourse in the narrative.

One more revolutionary figure of modern times, Albert Einstein, is often cited as a contributor to modernist thought. Not only did Einstein's *Theory of Relativity* encourage greater questioning of individual perspectives and of time, his scientific influences created, once again, both a public admiration for scientific and intellectual discovery and greater anxieties, particularly with his *Principles of Uncertainty*. Many modernist authors utilized his theories in support of their own. D. H. Lawrence used Einstein's concept of a world without absolutes to argue against imperialism, while Picasso presented Cubism as his interpretation of the concept of a world based on relativity. The notion of crossing vast distances at the speed of light encouraged both an enthusiasm for, and dread of, speed. Ultimately, as a result of Einstein's genius, the creation and use of the atom bomb encapsulated the paradox of modernity's advances. It is not any wonder that the public and writers became both fascinated with and horrified by the possibilities inherent in scientific study. For instance, Walker's *Medical Meeting*, written in the late 1940s, fictionalizes the solitary struggles of a scientist and doctor, Henry Baker, and his wife, Liz, as they search for a new strain of mold to assist ultimately in a cure for tuberculosis. Initially inspired by figures like the Curies and filled with a belief in scientific exploration, the characters of this 1949 novel discover the heartache and the dangers of such an enthusiasm for and single-minded faith in science. Written in the aftermath of Hiroshima in 1947 and 1948, during the public's fascination with and fear of scientific discovery, *Medical Meeting* should be read in light of the dark overtones of scientific advances.

Taking into consideration the recent critical revisionist work on modernism, particularly that of Peter Childs, this study will proceed by focusing on the pivotal influences of the above mentioned thinkers. The following discussion will study Walker's novels from an economic angle, in terms of Marx, and will focus on the effects of economic change on U.S. society, with its challenges to individual and community survival, the movement of the population from East to West and from the rural to the urban centers, coupled with an increasing consumerism and materialism of U.S. society. Moreover, the effects of Darwin's and Nietzsche's theories can be located in Walker's characterizations of the New Woman and the increasing secularization of American society. Freud's interest in the use of self-referentiality, memory, and dreams is addressed in the chapter on Walker's aesthetics. Saussure's theories on language and its unreliability are addressed in the discussions focusing on the novelist's quest for sharing meaning through literature. The effects of Einstein's theories on time and relativity inform the discussion examining Walker's use of alternating narrative perspectives, her use of psychological rather than chronological time, and her underlying anxieties concerning scientific exploration.

Although Walker utilized various linguistic devices to develop her themes, experimented in altering perspectives and chronological time, and even made references at times to mythology and classical literature in her prose, her writing never lapsed into the obscure and erudite style found in many traditional modernist texts. Perhaps due to this deceptively simple prose style, her works appear to have little in common with those of the high modernists. However, on just this subject, Elaine Jahner explains that Walker's work is anything but simplistic and that, in fact, her simplicity masks a very deep complexity:

> Twentieth century literature has been a grand experiment in what can be conveyed by way of stylistic high-wire acts. Walker's text does not belong to this tradition of stylistic experimentation. In all her writing, she stayed with simple

> language. Yet the simplicity of this work can be viewed as its strength as it tells an elemental American story about finding one's language, one's cognitive style in a definite landscape after migration [and modern displacement] has placed the individual where space no longer evokes the history that structures the rhythms of life. That is a process that requires clear telling, addressed to the general public. That is a narrative strongest in its impact when it is most directly told.
>
> [. . .] [T]he reader's perception of complexity might come only as an aftereffect, but it is no less real for all that. (Jahner 139–40)

Walker's unique modernist prose style originates from a variety of influences. Although she was well-educated and both studied and admired the works of Henry James and Virginia Woolf, her own upbringing in the household of a Baptist minister was very conservative, as was the environment she found herself in almost all her life. Circumstances both forced and allowed the novelist to discover other, less abstract forms of expression more natural to her own voice and landscape. For instance, although she did not write sentimental or romantic fiction, her invocations of nature and use of the natural world in her novels are trademarks of her work and can be easily mistaken for sentimental or romantic tropes. Even in her last novel, *The Orange Tree*, where she has a number of references to classical literature and mythological figures, the text still carefully balances obscure references to the ancient world and literature with "down-to-earth" descriptions of a fictionalized version of the landscape in and around her characters' Boston and Vermont landscapes, as if to somehow acknowledge the need for both texts and for their readers to find their own balance.

Perhaps if Walker's life had turned out differently—if she had found herself living in Europe or New York rather than Saginaw, Michigan, or Great Falls, Montana—her writing might have developed very differently. For instance, her first publication while she was still in college, an essay entitled "Gargoyles," demonstrates her early inclinations to high modernism with its obscure references to antiquities, its biting satire, and its outright criticism of Wells College administrators, who were outraged when they saw her depictions of "their limited lives" (Hugo 47). However, this "literary success," which resulted in both publication and a monetary prize, was shadowed by an ensuing lawsuit by these Aurora residents. Although the university quickly and quietly paid the settlement, one can only speculate about the chilling and long-term, self-censuring effects such an event had on this young writer. Although her subsequent fiction continued to critically examine the places and people she found herself in the company of, this early tendency toward criticism and satire in "Gargoyles" developed into seemingly more palliative texts that conveyed her opinions in increasingly complex fictional representations. The incident surrounding "Gargoyles" would also be the first and last time in the author's career that her writing would precipitate a lawsuit and such a public outcry.

Although she was raised in a relatively conservative environment, there is some evidence in letters, journals, and other biographical details that, given her own choice, Walker would have gravitated toward living in more liberal-minded and culturally oriented locations than she found herself in for much of her life. Certainly, throughout her career, her contemporary literary heroes tended to be the high modernists. Also, given that her later writing shows stronger elements of stylistic high modernism, it is reasonable to speculate that several life-altering events influenced the direction both she and her fiction would inevitably take.

Walker's marriage to the well-educated and culturally inclined Ferdinand Schemm may have led her to such a life, but the young family's direction was influenced by several events. The first was the Great Depression. With limited choices, the young Schemms took what work they could. In Doctor Schemm's case, this involved accepting a medical practitioner's position in a remote logging town on the Upper Peninsula of northern Michigan. Evidence of the isolation that a young, ambitious, and well-educated Mildred must have felt can be found in the fictional world of Celie in *Fireweed*. The trials of this young woman parallel the novelist's during those early years. As readers learn about the young woman's ambivalent feelings on marriage and young motherhood, they also catch glimpses of what this young writer must have felt being so isolated from the academic world of Wells College, where she had flourished. But living on the Upper Peninsula, surrounded by hard-working, straight-talking neighbors, may well have influenced, tempered, and even improved Walker's writing. The prose that emerged from this experience was clean, unaffected, and deceptive in its simplicity, as all her fiction would be. A certain detachment also complemented her sympathetic portrayal of the residents of her fictional Michigan landscape. This detachment is something she truly felt as an outsider peering into a world that she somehow knew would never be her own. Once again, this simultaneous detachment from and sympathetic portrayal of her characters and their stories would characterize all her fiction.

There are some parallels between what Matthew Bruccoli refers to as the "expatriate experience of American Modernists" and Walker's life within the continental U.S. Regarding Hemingway's experience, Bruccoli writes, "Expatriation supplied the isolation and time necessary for him to focus on his craft and develop his own vision and voice" (23). The same can be said for Walker. Walker found herself living in foreign environments, as did the expatriates. In moving to remote corners of the United States, she was exposed to people with cultures different from her own: Native Americans, immigrants, war refugees, and longtime residents of these areas who had maintained their own ethnic traditions. Bruccoli also notes that the expatriate experience exposed American modernists to new ideas and different cultures and people that were effective stimulants for creativity. Again, such was the case for Walker. Solitary for long hours, creative and observant, her own privately created fictional world became a necessity for her well-being and reflected her position in the new landscapes she resided within.

Bruccoli mentions that modernist writers often reacted to the expatriate experience with feelings of isolation and a detachment from the past and from family and traditional values, often separating young modernists from their Victorian-minded parents, creating orphan-like narrators. These feelings often created identity crises that led to processes of personal transformation and to passive, observational attitudes that, in modernist writing, often resulted in "the *dramatis personae* seeming more like spectators than participants in the action" (18). This detachment found its way into modernist writing in two ways: one in the dramatis personae reacting as spectators to the world around them; and the other in the narrators' presentations of their own lives and stories with almost the same distancing.

An example of this detachment can be found in a passage from Hemingway's *A Moveable Feast*, in which Hemingway explains how invigorating Paris was to him. However, he notes that in those early days, he did not write about the City of Lights or the people he met there. He wrote about northern Michigan and his own youth: "I had seen the end of fall come through boyhood, youth and young manhood, and in one place you could write about that better than another. That was called *transplanting yourself*, and it could be as necessary with people as other sorts of growing things" [my italics] (5). No doubt, Walker experienced this same "transplanting." For instance, she began to write *Fireweed* after she and her husband left Michigan and lived for four months in London. During this time, while her husband continued his medical education at St. Bartholomew's Hospital, she remained in their cold boarding house and worked on this manuscript. Her habit of writing about an environment that she was not immediately experiencing would continue for most of her career. For example, when the family moved from the Midwest to the West, she wrote many of her novels about the Midwest and New England. In fact, nearly ten years passed before the author wrote a novel that featured the physical landscape she occupied in the West. This was *Unless the Wind Turns*, written in 1941. But even in this novel, she still maintained her distance with her characters' relationships to the landscape. The characters are from the East, visiting Montana for a holiday. No doubt, at this point in her Montana residency, Walker still felt she was not fully part of this landscape and was therefore more at ease describing Montana from an outsider's point of view. It was not until *Winter Wheat* in 1944 that she created a character invested in a Montana landscape similar to her own. The creative achievement of this, her most popular novel, is her ability to both believably occupy the narrative sensibility of Montana-born Ellen, her protagonist, and also retain a certain measure of detachment. Perhaps because she had already resided in Montana for over a decade, had already written five novels at this point, and had perfected her narrative distancing to such a level, she was able to retain this professional distancing even in a novel so close to home. Interestingly, after *Winter Wheat*'s success, and at the height of her writing career and involvement in her Montana social life, the novelist again stepped away from this western landscape and wrote her historical Vermont novel, *The Quarry*. This novel is in many ways the story of her people, family, and community in New England and examines the erosion of a way of life that contributed to America's "westering"—and to her own.

Although Walker was relieved to move away from the Upper Peninsula of Michigan and back to Ann Arbor to continue her studies in English, the event that precipitated the move was undoubtedly the second event in her life that would eventually take her even further from artistic and intellectual centers that may still have redirected her interests and artistic sensibilities. While treating his patients in the logging camps, Ferdinand

Schemm suffered radium poisoning in his hand. Gangrene developed and several of his fingers were amputated. He would suffer recurring infections for the remainder of his short life. With his hoped-for career in surgery at an end, Doctor Schemm returned for further studies and a refocusing of his medical career in internal medicine at the University of Michigan. While Walker studied and wrote, her husband developed an interest in cardiology research. When the time came to set up his practice and with few options in a country still beset by the economic crisis of the Depression, he and Mildred had the choice of moving to Duluth, Minnesota; Portland, Oregon; or Great Falls, Montana. To Walker's initial dismay, Doctor Schemm believed Great Falls was the preferable location to establish his practice primarily because its residents seemed more open to new ideas and the existing medical community welcomed his research interests more so than in the other locales.

Even though most of the money for the move to the West came from Walker's award of the Avery Hopwood Prize and subsequent publication of what would be her first novel, *Fireweed*, it was prompted more by Ferdinand's enthusiasm than Mildred's. However, the financial success of *Fireweed* was the third major event in Walker's life that influenced her fiction and artistic inclinations. Although her initial literary leanings and interest in English, especially during her years in college, may well have been aesthetic and highbrow, her early economic success, coupled with her family's ongoing economic needs, altered the direction of her writing career. With the Avery Hopwood Award, not only did the young Schemm family have enough money to move west, they also had a guarantee by Harcourt Brace to publish *Fireweed* and two more novels. Walker was no longer writing solely for herself. Instead, she was balancing her aesthetic inclinations alongside the needs of her family and her publisher's expectations. This should not suggest that the author "sold out" for some lesser form of literature in order to create an income. However, these facts do indicate that she occupied a considerably more pragmatic realm than those writers who lived in poverty, on family stipends, or through private patronage, who were often freer to experiment and who wrote primarily for their own artistic needs and for their small coterie of admirers. To put it succinctly, as Ripley Hugo did in titling her mother's biography, Walker "wrote for her life," both literally and figuratively. She never wrote "potboilers," but arguably tempered her own aesthetic inclinations in response to her heightened awareness and appreciation of her readers' and publisher's interests.

After the success of *Fireweed* and the Schemm family's arrival in Montana in 1933, the young novelist was once again faced with cultural isolation in a community largely indifferent to her literary aspirations. In her own journals, written shortly after her arrival to the state, she describes her impressions of the country and its people:

> A ranch laid out on the flat prairie, a cluster of unpainted buildings without a tree or bush, so ugly it takes willpower to make yourself look at it. A women and two children, clothed in drab-colored garments, are guarding a fire of tumble-weed along the edge of the road. The fire leaps out of the dull background free, vivid, beautiful [. . .].
>
> [. . .] A man drives his tractor along the edge of his field while, on this side of the fence, walks his woman come to fetch him since it is too dark to work any longer. Both figures are bent, dumpy, wedded to the brown furrows, but escaping drabness because they are tied together [. . .]. (qtd. in Hugo: 139)

It is easy to imagine Walker's disappointment with this vast, plain, and drab world. However, in the entries that continue, the seeds of her own survival and growth as both a resident of Montana and an author are evident. Not only does she note the gray and the drab, but in equally great detail, she observes the hidden and potential beauty of the landscape. Her imagination and understanding of a more familiar landscape allow her to begin to make connections:

> These tiny wildflowers growing heedlessly out of the dry dirt of the flats are pure color: blue, such a bright yellow, red. They grow so low you might miss them easily. You feel them more than you see them [. . .].
>
> [. . .] A grain elevator standing up like an obelisk, functional but not beautiful, yet fitting, after a while, into the land; dominating the country around as cathedrals in the old world towns and as white-spired churches in the New England villages [. . .]. (qtd. in Hugo: 139)

Similar to the experience of the expatriate modernist writers, Walker found herself a foreigner in an alien land, and like these writers she was able to incorporate this foreign landscape and her heightened sensibility into her own fictional concerns and artistic representations. She began to inhabit and understand this place—alien as it was—by rendering her observations into words, an artistic process that was at the core of her work. Like fellow-Montanan Norman Maclean, Walker feels the land and life's apparent indifference to mankind begin to sing when she recognizes that it can be transformed into words.

Although Walker had several literary friends in Montana, such as journalist and historian Joseph Kinsey Howard and novelist A. B. Guthrie, her primary forms of literary connection and inspiration were with the printed word, which included letters from university friends and the weekly delivery of the Sunday edition of the *New York Times* and other periodicals. For much of her career Walker was not known as a novelist to the public or even to her own children, but was instead known as Doctor Schemm's wife. In part, this dual existence, once again very much paralleling the experiences of many modernist expatriates, may have also influenced her style, particularly in the sympathetic yet detached dramatis personae present in her fiction.

Bruccoli makes another point concerning the American expatriate experience that closely parallels Walker's life in the West. He discusses the difference between the American expatriates in Europe during the 1920s and the typical nineteenth-century expatriates. Bruccoli quotes *The Literary Review* of 1928: "'the average "exile" of today is living in France, or elsewhere in Europe, because he can live there'"—"because it is cheaper than living elsewhere," Bruccoli explains. "'By contrast, the typical nineteenth-century expatriate, unless a government or business employee, was more likely to belong to an affluent family'" (74). Similarly, the Schemms did not choose to move to the Rocky Mountain West in the 1930s for the same reasons that many affluent Americans do today; instead, they moved there because it was less expensive than other locales and seemed to have more opportunities. Largely, the nineteenth-century expatriates often gravitated to Europe searching for their own historical and cultural pasts, but the expatriates of the 1920s moved to Europe not for the past but for what they perceived as the increased possibility for engagement with current events and the future. Similarly, Doctor Schemm explained that he chose to move to Great Falls, Montana, with his family because it was "open to new ideas" and seemed to have a more robust future than the East. Living with these beliefs, Walker would have had a similar mindset to that of many modernist writers, with an eye to the future.

Yet another similarity between Walker's residence in remote locations in the United States and expatriates' lives in Europe merits attention. Bruccoli mentions that Hemingway believed that there was one very great danger in expatriate existence, despite all the artistic advantages in moving away from the outdated Victorian and Puritan ideals of America in the early part of the twentieth century. Without the discipline and constant reinforcement of the tenets of the Protestant work ethic ubiquitous in the day-to-day lives of U.S. residents, Hemingway observed that many expatriates fell into undisciplined lives of "dissipation and despair" (qtd. in Bruccoli: 79). Hemingway maintained that he did not fall into this "expatriate trap" because he adhered to his own deeply engrained work ethic and standards. Many other productive and successful modernist writers were also able to maintain their own standards despite the temptations in their environments to do otherwise. Certainly, the productivity, high literary standards, and professional success that Walker experienced during her twenty-two years of relative cultural isolation in Montana, in light of the fact that she too could have given in to a less disciplined work ethic and lifestyle, are examples of this modernist discipline. In fact, at only fifty, when she found herself a young widow, instead of turning to despondency and despair, she turned again to work.

Interestingly, within months of her husband's death, Walker sold the family's Montana home and returned to teach at Wells College. About this sudden departure, Ripley Hugo speculates that the family home was too much for her mother and too overwhelming with memories of the happy times with Ferdinand. Furthermore, her daughter explains that her mother did not want to become known around Great Falls as "the widow Schemm." Instead, she chose, this time solely of her own volition, to "transplant and transform." Although the "Montana years" were certainly the most professionally productive and successful for Mildred Walker Schemm and, the evidence suggests, the most personally satisfying, it remains tempting to speculate, in light of her rapid departure from the state after Ferdinand's death, whether she had not enjoyed those years largely because of their mutual interests and dedication to their family and home. In a sense, after her husband's death, Walker returned to the world she had occupied before her marriage, moving back to the seemingly more intellectually invigorating and culturally inclined world of Aurora, New York, to teach English at the very same campus she had attended as an undergraduate student twenty-nine years earlier. This return to a previous home was repeated when, upon retirement from teaching in 1968, she moved again, returning to her childhood home in Grafton, Vermont. Walker's movement helps to develop a fuller understanding of the author as a modernist writer. Her own life experiences, choices, and the subsequent arc of her literary concerns and production are inextricably entwined. Bruccoli mentions "fear of homelessness" as one of the synchronic issues of modernism. Although Walker was never without a home, per se, her fictional interest in the "fear of homelessness," issues of belonging, and her attention to her characters' reconciliations with foreign landscapes explain her own concerns and choices of residence, particularly in her years as a widow.

Her later writing, when she wrote far less out of financial necessity, is notably more experimental, but this experimentation in her later years certainly cannot be wholly attributed to economics. To be sure, Walker certainly hoped every one of her books would be well received, both publicly and critically. One might speculate that perhaps because she had spent nearly twenty of her later years in academia, this environment influenced her writing and resulted in greater stylistic experimentation and intertextuality. In contrast, in her earlier years in Montana she was Doctor Schemm's wife, involved in local events, raising children, and learning about Montana's working people that she visited while accompanying her husband on his house calls, and this environment influenced both the form and content of her fiction. Not surprisingly (to anyone except, ironically, Mildred Walker), her later fiction was considerably less well-received by the buying public than her earlier work; nonetheless, it also received some of Walker's highest critical acclaim. For instance, *The Body of a Young Man* did not sell well and marked her popular decline, but it also received one of her most prestigious literary recognitions—a nomination for the 1960 National Book Award. Although the novelist knew well how infrequently people read the authors she most admired, she was unable with her own work to separate her earlier, popular success and her later, more critical success from the notion of success and failure based on a capitalist system of monetary reward and public acclaim. No doubt, her career was further complicated by the fact that the publishing industry and public's taste in literature had changed over the course of her career. Evidence of this apparent change in the public's taste may be found in a letter Eleanor Roosevelt wrote after her second viewing of *The Southwest Corner*, performed on Broadway. The playwright, John Cecil Holm, who adapted Walker's novella to a script, wrote to Walker on March 6, 1955, that "Mrs. Eleanor Roosevelt saw the performance on Thursday night. She sent back word she thought it a fine and lovely play and that it was a reflection on the taste of the American audiences that the play was closing [after a month]. She thought it was a crime that it had to close" (qtd. in Hugo: 5).

3. The Aesthetics of Postmodern Modernism

The sensibilities of those we now refer to as the high modernists, marked by bold experimentation in both their lives and art and a self-conscious interest in form, were once the defining characteristics of modernists in general. However, for over four decades now literary critics have broadened both modernism's canon and its very conception, augmenting, altering, and at times completely eliminating these defining elements. Commencing with the revolt against New Criticism in the fifties and sixties, followed by the deconstructive schools of thought in the seventies and eighties, and more recently, postmodernism's preoccupation with modernism's sociopolitical context, literary critics have turned their focus from literary aesthetics to issues of race, gender, ethnicity, class, regionalism, and history. However, this broadening and liberalization of what was once considered a static canon and critical process developed by the New Critics risks overlooking and devaluing valuable critical work and insights of the past. Although much has been gained through a broadening of the modernist canon and an interdisciplinary integration of literature into other fields, many scholars, particularly those who were originally trained by teachers of New Criticism, still maintain a lingering uneasiness with solely accepting this new cultural interpretation of modernism. Despite their reservations, most contemporary critics still seem inclined to mention high modernist writers such as Gertrude Stein,

T. S. Eliot, and Virginia Woolf in their discussions, and only once the sociopolitical relevance of their author under study is compared to one or some of these high modernist writers will they proceed with their broader, new interpretations. Despite this tacit deference to the past, however, rarely do discussions of modernism focus solely on style and aestheticism, even though an examination of the author's style or aesthetic can yield valuable insights.

Walker's interest in and commentary on the events of modern life—her "diachronic approach," as Peter Childs would describe it—make studying her as a modernist writer, with a sociopolitical approach to her fiction, relatively straightforward. Regardless of how her texts are interpreted stylistically—or what political "side" the texts appear to align themselves with—her fiction is consistently in reaction to and in conversation with the people and events of her era and is arguably modernist. However, a more contentious, but nonetheless plausible, claim is to position Walker as a modernist writer in light of the criterion of the New Critics, the often high-wire stylistics of the high modernists, or the sensibilities of other, previously elite members of the canon.

In her afterword to *Women's Experience of Modernity*, Rita Felski writes, "What was distinctive and authentically modern in modernism—what allowed it to subsume the adjective into its own self-naming—was its bold and visionary use of form"—a form, she writes, that was often seen as subversive (290). "Subversive" is one of the original characterizations of high modernists. However, Hugh Witemeyer points out that a reading such as Felski's completely contradicts other interpretations that characterize modernists as conservative and occasionally even fascist, "attempting to uphold established order—[a] particularly capitalist order" (161).

Some clarification of these seemingly diametrically opposed definitions of modernism can be found in Astradur Eysteinsson's *The Concept of Modernism*. In his chapter "The Avant-Garde as / or Modernist?" Eysteinsson distinguishes between these two terms, which are often used incorrectly as synonyms, adding to the confusion over modernism's characteristics. He points out that although the two terms are "intimately related," "avant-garde" is most often "taken to be the subordinate term, which at the same time illustrates a central characteristic [and further complexity] of modernism" (141).

"Avant-garde," Eysteinsson explains, is not a term tied to any historical period but instead describes activities of an aesthetic characterized by the unconventional and experimental in both life and the arts. Because modernist literature was and still is often characterized by its unconventional nature and focus on experimentation, these two terms have understandably often been used interchangeably and are therefore confused with one another. Further complicating their distinction is the fact that the avant-garde lifestyles of artists such as H. D. (Hilda Doolittle), H. G. Wells, Virginia Woolf, Ezra Pound, Gertrude Stein, the Fitzgeralds, Edna St. Vincent Millay, and Dorothy Parker, seem ubiquitous to the modernist story.

According to Eysteinsson, the avant-garde was distinguished not only by its daring new artistic forms and lifestyles and violations of conventions and decorum but also by its self-consciously collective activities (144). This defining quality of the avant-garde is apparent in groups such as the Dadaists, the Futurists, the Cubists, the Bloomsbury Group, and more loosely in the Round Table at the Algonquin Club, at the various other venues in Greenwich Village throughout New York in the 1920s, and in the expatriate groups that gathered at Gertrude Stein's home and Sylvia Beach's Shakespeare and Company in Paris.

These avant-garde groups were also active in creating small presses and publication outlets that may not otherwise have been easily accessible for many of these artists. In London, Leonard and Virginia Woolf started Hogarth Press, which not only published their own work but also promoted modernist authors with the publication of Eliot's *Prufrock and Other Poems* and *The Waste Land* (Scott, *Refiguring Modernism* 113), selected works by Gertrude Stein (72), and translations of Chekhov and Dostoyevsky (68). In Paris, Sylvia Beach first published Joyce's *Ulysses*. Black Sun Press printed editions by D. H. Lawrence, James Joyce, and Hart Crane. Hemingway's original *In Our Time* first appeared thanks to William Bird's Three Mountains Press, also in Paris (67). The first editions of Gertrude Stein's *The Making of Americans*, H. D.'s *Palimpsest*, and Djuna Barnes's *Ladies' Almanac* were all published through Robert McAlmon's Contact Press (Bruccoli 65). Three Mountains Press, also in Paris, produced first editions of William Carlos Williams's *The Great American Novel* and selections of Ezra Pound's *Cantos*.

Pound insisted that these small presses were alternative not because the artists they featured could not find other, more popular venues, but because their private limited editions allowed artists to be more intimate and interesting to their exclusive group of readers (66). However, there are clearly other indications that these alternative presses were often the launching points for these artists' careers with popular presses. Based on his exposure to Hemingway's work through the small presses of Paris, F. Scott Fitzgerald encouraged the alliance between Hemingway and Scribner's, and when Stein's *The Autobiography of Alice B. Toklas*, originally published though the Plain Edition imprint, was chosen as a Literary Guild selection, she achieved her long-coveted attention from a New York publisher—Random House—with whom she retained her alliances for the rest of her life (67).

In *Ernest Hemingway and the Expatriate Movement*, Bruccoli speculates that "[t]he commitment of Random House to an avant-garde author such as Stein suggests how little magazines and small presses in Paris [and elsewhere] ultimately liberated publishers from their conservatism and transformed the American mainstream" (67). Although this might be true to some extent, and it may still be said of small presses today, Bruccoli's conclusion must be tempered with the fact that the tastes of the American mainstream did change and continue to do so—quite apart from encouragement by publishers, large or small. Furthermore, the ever-evolving style and interests of the avant-garde were by no means static as the years progressed. For instance, over the course of her career, Stein's style evolved from *Tender Buttons* and other highly experimental fiction to the more accessible prose her readers encounter in *The Autobiography of Alice B. Toklas*, which was and remains one of her most readable works.

This shift can be partly explained in light of the fact that in the evolution of their careers, modernists straddled a middle ground between the private patronage of the past and a cautious courtship with the free market. (For detailed examples of the economic challenges to modernists, see both Patrick Collier's essay "T. S. Eliot in the Journalistic Struggle" in *Challenging Modernism* and Bonnie Kime Scott's chapter "Becoming Professional" in *Refiguring Modernism: The Women of 1928*.) While many early modernist writers established their publishing careers with small presses, partially funded by private patronage and partially commercial, as many writers continue to do today, some also developed their careers via the increasingly critical role that universities began to play in the arts, which might be viewed as a continuation and evolution of the private patronage of the past. This alliance with academia is particularly common for the later modernists. Writers such as John Steinbeck studied at Stanford. Katherine Porter was a student in the University of Iowa Writers' program. Wallace Stegner's first novella, *Remembering Laughter*, achieved academic support through the Little Brown award, which entitled him to both a monetary prize and publication. Walker's writing career, because of her affiliation with the University of Michigan, was launched with her receipt of the Avery Hopwood award. However, acceptance and patronage from these various groups seems incongruous with modernists' individualism and separate accomplishments. Commenting on this apparent contradiction in "The Avant-garde as / or Modernism?" Eysteinsson writes: "This [group membership] feature of the avant-garde has even been used as a means of separating it from modernism. Most modernist canons [. . .] are selective groupings of individual talents, generally with heavy emphasis on isolated achievements rather than on historical production as a historical practice" (144). Eysteinsson further explains that the individual talents have proven more lasting than movements but maintains that the nature of the avant-garde as a "movement" is an underlying principle of modernism. Generally, avant-garde movements are seen as attempts to break, at times, from the present, the past, and / or the future, but modernism incorporates the concept of movement into its ideology as a bridging device that encourages the linking of the present to both the past and the future. "According to historical reconstruction," Eysteinsson writes, "the avant-gardes are primarily to be judged as the soil out of which sprouts the richer growth of Modernism and its masterpieces" (146). Some modernists—Eliot and Pound, for instance—can be seen as both breaking with the prevalent traditions (literary and otherwise) and also as salvaging fragments from the past. This is the bridge-like, fluid aspect of modernism. The avant-garde can be described as the cutting edge of modernism, an edge that, after it is created, fuses itself to modernism and disappears until it shows itself again, attempting to cut what was once its own embodiment. Because the two cannot be separated, Eysteinsson suggests, "[o]ne way to radicalize the concept of modernism fruitfully is to read modernist works from the perspective of the avant-garde" (177).

Following Eysteinsson's suggestion, a reader must then consider how a member of the avant-garde of the 1920s would have viewed Walker. Tongue-in-cheek, Ripley Hugo once asked her mother if she had been a flapper in the 1920s. Mention of the avant-garde brings to mind images like those from Marion Meade's *Bobbed Hair and Bathtub Gin: Writers Running Wild in the Twenties*, which at times reads like a handbook on abortion, affairs, and alcoholism. In this period the term "avant-garde" conjures up images of the publicly exposed homosexual affairs in Paris and New York, nights of drunken orgies, and highly experimental, tragic, and brave lives and artistic experiments. During those same years, Walker was living in the conservative home of a Baptist minister, attending prayer meetings and church socials, working diligently at school, going off to college on a scholarship, marrying a promising young doctor from an equally conservative midwestern family. If a member of the 1920s avant-garde were to follow the course of Walker's life, he or she would initially be confronted with all the trappings of the traditional conservative story of a middle-class, white, Anglo-Saxon Protestant woman. Furthermore, after the wild years of the 1920s, Walker didn't end her days in an asylum, kill herself, travel around the world, abandon her children, leave her spouse and run off with another man or woman, or discover that she suffered from liver poisoning, as many tragic figures did, particularly those portrayed in Meade's text. Instead, she lived in a quiet town in Montana with three children, preoccupied with the family's clothes, dinner parties, community fundraisers, her husband's work, and saving for what would become the single largest expense in the Schemm household: educating their children in tradition-laden institutions such as Yale and Amherst. This life hardly appears avant-garde. Isolated as she was for almost all her writing career—and quite apart from any apparent group or movement—Walker surely fell into the "high individualism" Eysteinsson describes in "Movements, Concepts and Masterpieces." However, her membership in the Junior League would seem to alienate her even further from any notion of the avant-garde. In light of Eysteinsson's suggestion that modernist works should be understood by reading them from the perspective of the defined avant-garde of the day, it hardly appears possible that any member of the 1920s avant-garde would have considered her a contemporary. However, when one reads Walker from the perspective of someone within the author's own social circle, this alternate approach creates a remarkably different interpretation of Walker's seemingly conservative life and work. Several times in Walker's biography, Ripley Hugo notes her mother's breaks from the conservativism that surrounded her. When Hugo describes her mother's summers spent in Grafton, Vermont, she writes, "I have come to think, she saw her parents in Vermont as more interesting than they were in the restricted world of parsonage boundaries and religious obligations" (2–3). Later, when describing her mother's entrance to Wells College on a scholarship, Hugo writes: "Attending College as a freshman in 1922 gave Mother the first of many opportunities to move her life in a different direction from her parents" (45). In these quotes a reader senses that Walker was constantly moving and pushing the edges of her own culture's restrictive boundaries. However, she did not move to the outside of her social circle and attempt to radicalize daily life and art, as an avant-garde artist might do, but instead remained within her own social circle, growing quietly and respectfully while still constantly pushing out on the inner edges of the cocoon of her pre-existing cultural boundaries. This quiet liberty-taking allowed for the possibility of not only a private metamorphosis but a gradual evolution of that entire social space.

Walker's quiet metamorphosis from within further illustrates Eysteinsson's distinctions between the avant-garde and modernism. The avant-garde of the early twentieth century came about in a period of history rife with revolution. Marxist thought, encouraging a "them against us" ethos that further manifested itself in an "either / or" mentality, was a theory embraced, in some matter or form, by many members of the avant-garde of this time. The avant-garde, strongly influenced by Marxism, reacted to modern life by attempting to remove itself from what it saw as its adversary: the establishment, the institutions, and the status quo. Many members of the avant-garde believed that they could achieve positive representation and change by removing themselves from the "inside" to a position on the "outside." But, as both Walker's novels and life demonstrate, reform is not necessarily most effective when existing systems are destroyed but is instead often more successful when amendments to the current systems and social order are encouraged, as they are in a constitutional democracy. This slow and quiet change from within an established system is not effectuated through revolution. Instead, change occurs through a quiet liberty-taking and growth. Still, the critical role that the avant-garde and radical members of society played and continue to play in the evolution and development of freedom and expression in a society ought not to be underestimated despite Walker's more conservative approach. In fact, in comparing the intentions of the avant-garde and modernists, it is apparent that their seemingly different attitudes toward modern life were more in their manners of approach to similar issues and goals than in the ends they sought. Neither group wished to uphold the status quo, and both were reacting to the same world events. As Eysteinsson points out, the avant-garde was often at the cutting edge of new attitudes and styles, and both the lives and art of its members played a crucial role in modern culture. It would be an oversight to ignore the avant-garde in the context of twentieth century studies, but it would equally be a mistake to overlook the movement's quiet contemporaries.

Although Walker's liberty-taking might have appeared mild and nonthreatening to the avant-garde in Paris in the 1920s, an approach with this interpretation is misleading and is perhaps the wrong perspective from which to judge Walker's life and work. It may well be more appropriate to study Walker by asking how her grandmother or neighbors would have viewed her lifestyle and fiction. Hugo writes, "Mother's stories about her college years suggested to my brothers and me how colorful she must have been [. . .]" (46). A reader must wonder, "colorful" in relation to whom—to the people around her? For example, Walker described how in school plays she wore a thick flannel bathrobe that her mother had made especially for her to take to college. Considering her background, it was tradition-breaking and radical to take a warm robe that had been lovingly sewn by her caring mother and stuff it in the bottom of a trunk, only to bring it out as a costume. Again, when she married, she agreed to do so only under the proviso that she would never have to do laundry and dishes. Within her community of laboring women, her neighbors in northern Michigan (fictionalized in *Fireweed*) in the 1930s, her proviso to never do laundry and dishes would have seemed absolutely radical.

In *Writing for Her Life*, Hugo attempts to study and understand what she describes as these two separate lives her mother lived: the public life as a wife and mother, and the secretive and private life as a writer and successful business woman. In Hugo's passage there is also a questioning of the seemingly incongruous reactionary and radical aspects of her mother's life and work:

> In writing this family memoir of my mother, I have been keenly aware of the two lives that she always led: the one, essential to her sense of well-being; the other, essential to the strength and excitement of her writing. She kept the dimensions of her life as a wife and mother separate from the more daring dimensions of her life as a writer. I have come to believe that she took few risks and asked few questions of her life as a doctor's wife because she could do that brilliantly and safely in her life as a writer. I think that dichotomy has a part in the strangeness my brothers and I felt—that we were not included in her writing life because we fulfilled a role in her nonwriting life. (xix)

Why Walker separated these lives as she did poses interesting questions. Perhaps she felt that if she fused these two lives, and if her own family and neighbors read and discussed her books, she could not have pressed on the boundaries of her own culture as freely as she did in her private world of letters. Or, perhaps she was concerned that public knowledge of her somewhat untraditional life might make her the subject of gossip and ridicule, as it did for many of her novels' characters. Additionally, she may have believed that some members of her own community were similar to the neighbors she depicted in Brandon Rapids, Montana, who felt threatened by the iconoclastic Pamela Lacey in *A Curlew's Cry*, or by the hypocritical suffragettes in *The Brewers' Big Horses* who outrightly criticized Sara Henkel for attempting to work in a man's world, or by the gossipy neighbors in *Light from Arcturus* who saw only selfishness in Julia Hauser's desire to move her family from their mercantile business in a safe and quiet Midwest town to the bright lights and culture of Chicago. Walker may have separated her thoughts that appear regularly in her novels from her everyday life because she, in fact, saw herself in these ostracized and misunderstood characters and was wary of their plights. Furthermore, she may have been concerned that departing from the norms of her social circle could possibly be interpreted as a threat to her family, friends, and identity as Mrs. Schemm, the doctor's wife. All in all, her complicity within the social sphere that she quietly criticized indicates her belief in a slow and non-radical metamorphosis from within as opposed to a more dramatic and revolutionary form of radicalism traditionally typifying the avant-garde.

In her biography, Hugo cannot help but wonder how Walker reconciled her art with her life. It is, in fact, Hugo who gives, perhaps unknowingly, the answer to this question. In the introduction to her mother's biography, Hugo describes how she and her other family members still wonder when they read her novels how the conservative woman they knew would have been interested in the characters in these books. She suggests, "I expect that [question] would have been a matter of indifference to Mother. It was a novel of hers, not her literary persona that she wanted understood" (xxi). The reconciliation Hugo seeks and the basis of her mother's modernist sensibility are to be found here in Hugo's own words. What was most important for Walker, the novelist, was not the reality of actual day-to-day life, nor how the world would view her life relative to her art, but her art alone. In her life, this attempt to separate her art from her life is indicative of the fragmentary nature of modernism itself. Her form of modernism is not an aesthetic that attempts total resolution or reconstruction between life and art but is instead an earnest attempt to find understanding in art alone.

On one level, Walker was a storyteller with her novels, often very realistic in her narrative depictions. Modernism, however, seemed "to go against the very notion of narrativity, narrative progression, or storytelling," Eysteinsson notes in his essay "Realism, Modernism, and the Aesthetics of Interruption" (187). Eysteinsson discusses examples as far-ranging as the works of Joyce, Kafka, Faulkner, and Balzac. However, he concludes that even in these texts that require the most decoding and seem the least reader-friendly, readers are still most likely to decode these based upon the cultural systems from which they operate in attempts to create "a story." Therefore, regardless of the fragmentary and experimental nature of the texts, readers inevitably interpret and adapt them to the very system of predictability the texts attempt to avoid. Eysteinsson notes further variations of realist fiction, distinguishing the nineteenth-century novel from the modern realist novel. As a generalization, social realism, most characteristic in "the predominant literary doctrine of eastern Europe since the mid-forties in the Soviet Union" with its use of a central consciousness and the presentation of a complete social order (179), can be distinguished from modernist fiction's drift from this portrayal of a social whole to its alternate presentation by the use of a personal consciousness. Eysteinsson also suggests that modernists often actually used the guise of the traditional realist narrative form to concomitantly offer readers seemingly traditional stories and to raise questions concerning realism's veracity within these novels' subtexts. Examples of such duplicitous employment include Fitzgerald's Nick Caraway in *The Great Gatsby* and Cather's Jim Burden in *My Ántonia*. Virginia Woolf also attempted to distinguish modernism from realism by (somewhat highhandedly and rashly) claiming that the older version of realism was written by what she termed "materialists," writing of unimportant things, whereas Georgians like herself found more important material by looking inside even an ordinary mind on an ordinary day. Discounting her broad claim, there is some truth in Woolf's comment that clarifies the distinctions between the older forms of realism and the modernists' version. Woolf's use of psychological realism, unreliable narrators, and fragmented presentations of time distinguish her works from their predecessors.

Although Walker utilized these modernist techniques, her writing style never appears as dense, convoluted, or complex as those of many other modernists; however, she certainly was not alone in this regard. For instance, Ernest Hemingway's work is noteworthy for its clarity and simplicity, going much against the grain of the stylistically complex works of authors like Joyce and Faulkner. In fact, Hemingway's fiction is best known for its simplification through omission and compression, qualities that also characterize Walker's novels. On this matter of style, Hemingway wrote: "If a writer of prose knows enough about what he is writing about he may omit things that he knows and the reader, if the writer is writing truly enough, will have a feeling of those things as strongly as though the writer had stated them. The dignity of the movement of an iceberg is due to only one-eighth of it being above water" (Hemingway, *Death in the Afternoon* 92). One sample of modernist omission and compression that is often used as an example of what was not being said appears in Hemingway's "Hills Like White Elephants," where in a short and nonsensical conversation, it is apparent to all readers that the man and woman are discussing a pregnancy, an abortion, and possibly a break up, although none of these topics are ever mentioned explicitly. Readers find a similarly abbreviated narrative in the fractured conversations between Lucy and Phyllis in Walker's *The Body of a Young Man*, discussed later in this chapter. Additionally, Cather, like Hemingway, expected a reader to help in the creation of the text. Because all these writers endowed their characters with human qualities and because these were qualities readers could also sympathize with, there was ample room for these readers to participate in the creative process and to appropriate the texts as their own.

Walker also employed the poetic device of literary compression through the use of symbolism and juxtaposition, as did many of her modernist predecessors and contemporaries. Her choices of poetic compression inherent in her works are examples of modernist experimentation, despite their deceptively simple and realist appearance. Often in her novels readers must gather the pieces of the story from dialogue alone. The scenic descriptions are also often fragmentary, and readers, again, must paint the fuller picture. Eysteinsson claims that the High Modernist texts, which in some ways demand decoding by their readers, are often counterproductive to their own ends—of waking their readers to a new sense of cultural possibility—because they are antithetical to the principle of rhetoric in fiction. Therefore, by offering a more palatable text with an appearance of totality and an adequate amount of a traditional narrative so that readers were not frustrated or intimidated by their novels—as they sometimes were by the stylistics of some of the high modernists—many other modernists were able to create greater sympathies with their readers than was sometimes the case with more radical works of fiction. In this way, seemingly popular language, with its many layers of meaning both expressed and implied, was and is able to engage in the practice of cultural criticism in normative communicative language, the language of realist fiction. Eysteinsson suggests that modernism which looks and reads like realism employs many of realism's tools; however, it extinguishes the false appearance of totality that characterizes some earlier works of realism through its fragmentation of description, dialogue, and language itself.

David Lodge offers a fuller explanation of how modernist writers differentiated their work from that of their predecessors. In his essay "The Language of Modernist Fiction: Metaphor and Metonymy," Lodge examines modernists' use of metaphors and other poetic devices by discussing a linguistic study done by Roman Jacobson entitled "Two Aspects of Language and Two Types of Aphasic Disturbances." Jacobsen believes that language (whether spoken or written) involves two operations: first, selecting linguistic units, and second, arranging these units. Through the process of selection, substitution and therefore the use of metaphor are possible. Lodge writes that metonymies are "the figures which name an attribute, adjunct, cause or effect, instead of the things itself and are closely related to synecdoches (part standing for the whole—or whole standing for the part)." He concludes that Jacobsen "discounted the traditional rhetorical theory that metaphor and metonymy should fall under the same general heading of tropes and figures" and concluded that "in normal verbal behavior, both processes are continually operative but [. . .] under the influence of a cultural pattern, personality and verbal style, preference is given to one of the two processes over the other" (483).

From this, Lodge draws a parallel conclusion about a wide range of modern artistic productions. He argues that because modernist fiction has a symbolist bias, it should tend to rely upon the use of metaphor. He then cites that there is a statistically higher use of metaphor found in modern fiction than in realist works. By way of example, he offers the titles of a number of novels categorized as realist, where their authors tended to use the names of places and people, with titles such as *Kipps*, *New Grubb Street*, and *The Forsythe Saga*. He then mentions some of the novels considered modernist—*A Passage to India*, *Finnegan's Wake*, *The Rainbow*, *To the Lighthouse*, and *Ulysses*, all indicative of their authors' use of substitution and similarity—and suggests that the use of metaphor in *Finnegan's Wake* is at such an extreme end of the metaphoric pole and so lacking in metonymic form that it is considered an "unreadable" modernist novel by many.

Lodge then follows the arc of Gertrude Stein's writing, which is considered a prime example of modernist experimentation with her tendency toward both the metonymic and metaphoric poles. He notes that her earlier work was notable for its use of metonyms, while later in her career, she tended toward the metaphoric pole when her writing had been arguably influenced by the early work of Hemingway. Lodge offers an example of Hemingway's work and demonstrates how his use of contiguous relationships and a synecdochic presentation of material allowed him to be both realist and symbolist.

In the following quote from "In Another Country," Hemingway offers an example of these contiguous relationships. However, his substitution of such images as "cold" and "fall" for the war indicates a use of metaphor as well. Lodge believes that Hemingway's metonymic style in the following is made to serve the purposes of the metaphor:

> In the fall the war was always there, but we did not go to it any more. It was cold in the fall in Milan and the dark came very early. Then the electric lights came on, and it was pleasant along the streets looking in the windows. There was much game hanging outside the shops, and the snow powdered in the fur of the foxes and the wind blew their tails. The deer hung stiff and heavy and empty, and small birds blew in the wind and the wind turned their feathers. It was a cold fall and the wind came down from the mountains. (qtd. in Lodge: 490)

Lodge concludes by suggesting that "if the initial trigger-mechanism of memory is metaphoric, the expansion and exploration of any given memory is essentially metonymic" (493) and that "if an essentially metaphoric mode of writing can utilize metonymy in this way, it follows that the basically metonymic mode of traditional realism can make extensive use of the metaphor"—hence, the modernist style (494).

Poet and scholar Sharon Bryan also comments on some of these same stylistic adaptations in direct reference to Walker's fiction. In Bryan's introduction to *The Body of a Young Man*, she writes that the novel "borrows many of its techniques from poetry: the compression, the layered imagery, the flair for the illuminating metaphor [. . .]. Reviews of the first edition mention Hemingway [. . .]" (vii). Although, on first glance, Walker's fiction appears simple, straightforward, and often traditionally realist, like its creator, it pushed at the boundaries of both contemporary culture and traditional novelistic forms, encouraging readerly interpretations that bridged the past to the future and questioned its own effectiveness in doing so. Closer readings reveal considerably more unstable and self-reflective subtexts. Similar to the works of Willa Cather, Walker's fiction can be read on two very different levels; if readers limit their interpretations to surface appearances and storylines, they overlook considerable value and inherent complexity.

Similarly, Cather's fiction was, until recently, often dismissed as being "simplistic," "sentimental," and "romantic." However, with new approaches to modernist literature, particularly those initiated through feminist and postmodern studies, the misreading of the romanticism and simplicity in Cather's novels has been and continues to be replaced with interpretations doing justice to her work's complexity and bold experimentation. For example, in *Willa Cather's Modernism*, published in 1990, Jo Ann Middleton demonstrates Cather's modernist sensibility. Although Middleton's work, with its suggestion to re-read Cather in a new critical light, appears somewhat dated today in light of all the recent work in Cather studies and the heightened appreciation and careful readings that organizations such as the *Cather Society* and the *American Association Society of Women Writers* have produced, her text still points to a problematic area in modernist studies. Middleton cites numerous examples of critics who still question how Cather could have been as far-removed from the avant-garde movements of her time. Middleton offers the following comments as evidence of the continued misreading of Cather's *oeuvre* and of the general distinction between the avant-garde and modernists:

> Why then, didn't the avant-garde look to Willa Cather, as they did to Gertrude Stein, for guidance and inspiration? First, Cather's work appeared too simple and clear, too easily understood; complexity was integral to modernists. Second, they must have believed that Cather was too popular a writer to be very good; a certain elitism marked the new breed of writer. Third, Cather's subject matter seemed nostalgic, her style seemed romantic, and her respect for tradition seemed old-fashioned to those revolting against nineteenth-century literary conventions. (37)

Certainly, everything that is said here of Cather's fiction could be said of Walker's. Like Cather's fiction, Walker's simple and clear writing can be read as more complex and duplicitous in its nature than the most outwardly stylistic and experimental texts. Middleton also distinguishes highbrow art from lowbrow art by noting that if a novel were popular to the mass market, a New Criticism reading would imply that it surely could not have been modernist—an indication of the elitism and isolation that certain groups of the avant-garde supported, which has resulted in confusing the exclusive and limited nature of the term "modernism." Furthermore, although both Walker's and Cather's fiction often appear somewhat nostalgic and romantic, this is yet another duplicitous aspect of their writing. Both the future and the past fascinated them, as it did most modernists. However, what most distinguished Cather as a modernist writer, Middleton claims, was her interest in the novel (not its subject matter) as an evolving form and her experimentation with that form—not experimentation for experimentation's sake, but as an organic reaction to the subject matter and theme of a particular work and an authorial attempt to reconcile form and concept. Middleton suggests, "Cather actively tried a new approach with each book, and each book dictated its own experiment" (41). Again, the same can be said of Walker. Although throughout her life Walker read with interest the works of James, Woolf, Chekhov, Cather, and many other contemporary writers and admired their work, her style was her own. Her journals are filled with both her own thoughts and quotes by many well-known modernists concerning the technique of writing, particularly the novel, the idea of an organic whole, and the concept of form-oriented versus content-oriented writing. By her own admission she began not with a story but with a character at a particular point in his or her life, and this fact exemplifies her modernist sensibility. She did not embark on the writing of a novel to tell a story. The story in fact was merely a vehicle to deliver her characters' concerns to readers in an approachable and manageable form.

Perhaps the best example of Walker's concern with form and perspective is in her decision to rewrite *Winter Wheat*. At the last minute the novel was rewritten from a third–person perspective to the limited first-person perspective of Ellen Webb, the unreliable and constantly changing young protagonist. This novel would have been entirely different if it had been told through the words of an omniscient narrator or from another character's perspective. Readers might not have been as receptive to the mixed messages in this text if they had not been conveyed by this vacillating and endearing young voice. This unreliable narrator is granted privileges that an older or omniscient narrator would not have been as likely to receive. For instance, Ellen begins by thinking that her parents don't even know what love is and that their marriage was primarily one of necessity. Although readers can sympathize with Ellen's opinions, they can also see beyond her young and confused thoughts and misunderstandings and, in doing so, derive a feeling of satisfaction in their knowledge that they know a bit more than the immature narrator. This choice of narrative device creates a readerly sympathy for her instability—and for the text's.

Even in her last novel, *The Orange Tree*, Walker continued to agonize over how to present the narrative, often rewriting entire sections either from the perspective of the younger or older female protagonist. In her final draft she decided to have the various characters share a place in the narrative. Because the central consciousness, Tiresa, dies before the novel concludes, the narrative required another central consciousness. The author overcame this narrative dilemma by rewriting entire sections of the text, giving limited narrative sensibilities to both Olive and Paulo. Although these characters never have the full narrative freedom that Tiresa has in the text, they are given enough to share some of their thoughts, to further destabilize the text, and to continue to engage readers and to perpetuate a readerly sympathy throughout the remainder of the novel. Walker's use of this split narrative sensibility also creates a fragmented sense of reality; readers are able to partake in several different observations and reactions to the very same events. This approach is characteristic of many of Walker's novels, and it allows her readers to debate freely the reality of the situations and also to question why certain details are relevant to one character and not to another. The vacuoles—or iceberg effect—of what is not observed and what is unspoken serve many of her works. For instance, in the conclusion of *The Orange Tree*, when each character confronts Tiresa's death, it is obvious that the thoughts and feelings of Paulo and Olive are completely disparate despite their earnest attempts to share in this mutual grief.

The instability and unreliability of language that characterize modernist texts was a constant concern of Walker's and appears repeatedly in her novels through the thoughts of her characters. One such example of this occurs with Harriet Ryegate in *If a Lion Could Talk*, who discusses the breakdown of communication openly in her journal when she and her husband return from an unsuccessful attempt to convert the Native Americans along the upper Missouri to Christianity. As Harriet sees her husband off, estranged from him because of their breakdown in communication and closeness, she thinks "[h]ow stupid she had been, insisting that they must talk everything out, always say what they meant, when they themselves couldn't always know" (265).

Throughout Walker's novels, characters are constantly second-guessing the actions and words of others. For instance, in *Dr. Norton's Wife*, the protagonist, Sue Norton, has literally lost her ability to communicate through the debilitating effects of multiple sclerosis. By using this character as the central consciousness, the author once again studies the breakdown of communication, both literally and figuratively. In this novel, each character begins to read different meanings into the smallest actions or silences until no one is operating on the same plane of understanding and the seemingly ordered household is underpinned by a silent and swirling chaos of misinterpretations and second-guessing. By witnessing what is not said, or hearing the tone of what is expressed rather than the words themselves from her hospital bed, Sue Norton attempts to relate others' discomfort and frustration to her own situation. As her health diminishes, Sue also believes she detects a quietly growing affair between her husband and sister. Furthermore, although her husband, in order to save her the pain, does not tell her that her disease cannot be arrested, his kind silence causes her even greater pain. Ironically, what is withheld and what could easily have been articulated and corrected is not. Instead, stammered and broken lines are the only feeble attempts any of the characters are able to articulate in an attempt to express what perhaps can never be said about love and death. In this novel's study of frustrated communication, readers once again sense the modernist writer's concerns about the overall value and reliability of language.

The Body of a Young Man also presents some of Walker's most tortured figures, who suffer from the breakdown of communication. The novel, like *Dr. Norton's Wife*, has a loose storyline in which very little happens on the surface. In *Dr. Norton's Wife*, Sue Norton is an invalid in bed when readers first meet her, and she remains so as the novel closes. She literally has hardly moved, and seemingly, no one else has either. The characters still go through their day-to-day routines, but the actual story and drama have largely been contained in their minds and emotions, as they are again in *The Body of a Young Man*.

Bryan points out in her introduction to this novel that "[m]uch of the pleasure here comes from reading between the lines. The novel is propelled not by dramatic events, but by subtler internal shifts that more often shape our lives" (vi). Bryan points out that the most obviously dramatic event in the book has already taken place offstage—the suicide of James's high school student that prompts the family to get away from home and visit old friends for the summer (vi). Once again, this novel's attention is not focused on the story itself but in the exploration of the characters' attempts and failures to communicate and create a sense of unity out of this tragic event. In her introduction to the novel, Bryan points out, moreover, that although the thematic focus in *The Body of a Young Man* is on friendship and change, the author's interest is once again in studying the incongruities between what is perceived and what is actual. This text exemplifies Walker's modernist sensibility, which questions the unreliability of the past vis-à-vis the present, as if to say that what worked once does not work now, and that people should let the past be just that.

In *The Body of a Young Man*, Walker seriously questions some of the literary devices that she employs regularly in many of her novels. For instance, in her earlier novels—and even in *The Body of a Young Man*—the author often uses metaphors as a form of poetic compression. The metaphors that appear consistently throughout her novels are arguably made even more apparent in this text. Metaphors extend from her first novel, with the fireweed symbolizing rebirth, through to her later work, where winter wheat becomes the physical embodiment of hope. Again, in the first paragraph of *The Body of a Young Man*, readers find poetically rich and metaphoric opening lines: "The road curved so often there was no clear view ahead. It twisted on itself in wide loops [. . .], but it was still so narrow that ferns and witch grass brushed against the side of the car, and there was no place to turn and go back" (3). Metaphorically, the road that the friends travel down is the journey back into a friendship that they intend to renew under new circumstances. Once they begin this journey there is no returning. The sunless green hollows represent aspects of themselves that they will find they cannot share with each other. The maidenhead ferns and witch grasses included in this passage create a feeling of claustrophobia and foreboding for readers that the characters will suffer throughout the text.

The narrator deliberately has these metaphors continue to emerge in the thoughts of both the central characters, Phyllis and Lucy. At times in this novel, it is almost tempting to accuse Walker of overusing the metaphor, particularly through the incident with the loom, when Phyllis's weaving project is stained by the children's spilled red paint, and also in the capture of a raccoon. These metaphors appear almost obvious and overwrought. Lucy considers her work at the loom her private act of creation apart from the family. The weaving, according to Phyllis, symbolizes a woman's attempt to create patterns, order, and beauty out of life's loose and untidy strands. The red stain from the paint, dripping from the eaves of the old New England barn, summons notions of original sin and the Puritan belief in man's inherent flaws.

It is important to note that these and the other metaphors of thick forests, sad rain, and deep cold pools are considered in the interior dialogue of the novel's tortured characters and not by the narrator. Interestingly, despite the novel's seemingly rich use of metaphors, the narrator allows—even encourages—a questioning of the value of these metaphors relative to the characters' varying interpretations of them. For instance, with each character's unique interpretation, according to his or her individual needs, of the mysterious release of the raccoon, the text brings to the reader's attention the instability and uselessness of these interpretations. Because all these characters are literary-minded—even the children are walking through the text reading *Great Expectations* and other classics—no one fails to see the caged wild raccoon as the living embodiment of everyone's tension. However, Walker carefully demonstrates how each character utilizes this same metaphor differently. By doing so, the narrative creates a greater self-reflective instability. The metaphors' significance and constructive purposes are questionable when it is apparent that they can have a myriad of misleading meanings. The characters' questioning of the use of the metaphor causes a more general, subtextual questioning of the value of the metaphor in fiction. Although this implicit questioning appears to destabilize the text, it does not do so completely. A line is drawn here that distinguishes this modernist text from its postmodern successor.

Walker's protagonist uses the metaphor against itself again in *The Orange Tree*. At one point in the novel, Tiresa wryly comments to her husband that at least they had taught their young friend to use "the metaphor." This comment is ironic both because Tiresa herself employs metaphors in her private reveries and conversations and, in turn, because the novelist utilizes them to create her text. The self-consciousness of this fragile poetic construction is implicit in Tiresa's comment. The author's own rendering of reality and use of metaphors is again under scrutiny at the end of the novel when the central symbol, the orange tree, comes under closer examination. To Tiresa, the novel's primary character, the little orange tree that stands on her balcony is a living symbol and reminder of the happy times that she and her husband shared in Sicily. As she approaches her own death, Tiresa comes to see the orange tree as the essence of the love between her husband and herself and as something that will survive her own existence. However, upon her death, the tree is only a tree to the remaining characters. It is clear by the end of the novel that its significance lay only in the fact that Tiresa placed this meaning upon it and shared that signification with her survivors. By employing this orange tree as a metaphor and once again demonstrating how personal and contrived the metaphor can be, Walker employs what Eysteinsson refers to as "normative communicative language" (208). The metaphor in this case demonstrates that reproducing the symbolic order is not necessarily an act of uncritical assent. In essence, Walker turns her own narrative, created by unreliable narrators, upon itself. In doing so, she is still able to maintain what on the surface appears as a realist narrative, but in fact she creates a text that, on the subsurface, questions its own methodologies and is self-reflectively modernist.

Walker's crisis of self-worth that she suffered as a writer, and her questioning the value of the years she dedicated to trying to create meaning from words, were not unique to her but were characteristic of many modernist writers, particularly in the later years of their careers. Although Walker questions the meaning of words and veracity in all her work, in her later novels, especially her last three—*The Body of a Young Man*, *If a Lion Could Talk*, and *The Orange Tree*—the crisis and negativity are most apparent. These novels still maintain a superficial, normative narrative construction, but their instability is apparent in the prevalent use of flashbacks, unordered time sequencing, split perspectives, and alternating central consciences. For instance, *The Body of a Young Man* repeatedly contrasts the perceptions and reactions of Phyllis with those of Lucy, to the very same situations. In one scene, as the two women walk down a New England street, Lucy comments, "Isn't this street lovely? You know, I've been here every summer of my life." Phyllis responds, "Lovely. It makes me think of *Little Women*." The text then reads: "Lucy tested the remark in her mind, wondering just how Phyllis meant it" (30). Later, when Phyllis sees her husband "sitting with a book and not reading it, [it] would make her aware that he had retreated again to that place in his mind where he didn't take her." But when Lucy sees James in that same demeanor, she assumes he is still brooding over the loss of his student and simply needs a distraction (46). Again, when the two women go for a swim, the novel captures another example of instability in communication. In one passage, Lucy and Phyllis are swimming and idly chatting, but beneath the surface, a tension builds, and Walker writes that the women "were both skipping sentences now, on the surface" (97). In this complex and highly charged scene, readers get a glimpse of what Sharon Bryan, in her critical introduction to the novel, calls "the poetic condensation" of the narrative, which occurs in what is and is not said and how the characters' movements and observations can be interpreted as either contributing to or further confusing the communication process. The text seems insistent in including the lines "They were both skipping sentences now" specifically for readers who might not have already ascertained this.

Throughout the novel Lucy is portrayed as the steadier and more solid of the two women, living in the world of earthly pleasures, weaving with her hands and gardening. Lucy has memories of her mother on the same property where she currently resides. In contrast, readers learn that Phyllis and her husband have always lived in rental homes. Of the two women, Lucy is certainly more like part of the rock that they sunbathe on in this scene. In contrast, Lucy wonders how Phyllis can be content passing her free hours by walking and reading, rather than participating in more earthly pursuits. Initially, Phyllis appears to be the more troubled character, the woman who lives more in the world of thought and the one who, in response to Lucy's idle comment about becoming part of the rock, remarks vehemently that she wishes she could be the wind. When the conversation gets too heavy for Lucy, she literally takes the weight from her head by unpinning her hair and dropping down into the pool. At this point in the scene, Phyllis directs her comments to matters concerning her husband, as though to explain to Lucy that her worries about him are the sole reason for her anxieties. Once again, Lucy sees through this and will not allow Phyllis to hide behind her husband and his worries. She says in response to Phyllis, "Jim adores you." The narrator asks the reader to consider how the women shift abruptly from talking about rocks and wind to discussing their marriages. Only in the second half of the novel does Phyllis come to realize the full import of Lucy's seemingly irrelevant remark. The fact that Lucy immediately perceives what is truly troubling Phyllis and the fact that Phyllis cannot hear her friend's message is the crisis that drives the latter half of the novel. Although Phyllis claims and actually believes she has visited her husband's old friends with the pretense of improving his emotional and mental state after the suicide of one of his students, she in fact has come to them because it is her marriage and her own security that worry her.

Throughout the novel, even the most innocent remarks become charged with second meanings that are often misconstrued. Led through this psychological warfare, a reader begins to sense that these characters might in fact be closer to understanding the situation if they tried to construct less out of what they have heard. Late in the novel, as Phyllis is preparing to leave, she and Lucy walk together for one last swim and have a final fragmented and confusing conversation. Similar to the previous chat earlier at the swimming hole, their thoughts skip as they talk about their children, their husbands, and the weather. Lucy concludes by saying "It's [the water's] going to be cold." In the next line, the narrator adds: "Each sentence seemed to stand alone, not lead on to the next one" (175).

Certainly, the text in *The Body of a Young Man* vacillates between the metaphoric and metonymic poles described by David Lodge. Walker's novels typically offer contiguity between one event and the other, but in the case of the fragmented discourse the women have on the way to the pool, a reader must rely almost wholly on the metaphoric implications of what is being said since one thought does not seem to flow from the previous one. Phyllis herself again wonders, as she has throughout the novel, about communication and one sentence standing alone—having no relation to the next. However, when faced with this metonymic breakdown, the women continue to walk to the pool. The pool is the physical embodiment and symbolic site of the linguistic breakdown, and going there returns them metaphorically to the site of the drowning suicide of the young boy. This death did not logically follow the course of events in the families' minds or lives. The boy had a scholarship to study physics at an Ivy League university, and there seemed no rational reason why, having worked so hard and achieved so much, he should have taken his life. It could be said that his act of suicide defied the metonymic ordering of life events. Left with this chaos, the friends have only the metaphor to cling to in helping them comprehend the incomprehensible. But, given that the text has already questioned the usefulness of the metaphor and that the author has suggested the same for her readers subtextually, the site of the confusion, the inexplicable death, and the linguistic breakdown become one and the same. In this passage in particular, readers sense that Walker presents her story by failing at the metonym while concomitantly relying upon and questioning the weakness of the metaphor—destabilizing her own creation while successfully and simultaneously upholding it. Her narrative continues for her readers, just as the women continue to walk despite their seemingly senseless conversation.

In creating these intelligent and overwrought characters who have much in common with modernists searching for epistemological absolutes, Walker makes a statement about both readerly and writerly texts and their interpretations. However, she does this within the context of a modernist text itself, once again demonstrating literature's ability to be both self-referential and unfixed, a complex modernist notion she carried forward in both her life and aesthetic.

4. The Economics of Modernism

In *New Women, New Novels: Feminism and Early Modernism*, Ann Ardis presents a widely held interpretation of how modernists meld their styles and attitudes: "The modernists—if not initially, then certainly by 1922—presented their reactionary politics as apolitical formalism, insisting upon the dissociation of art from the rest of culture" (171). In the late 1980s revisionist postmodern work advocating an expansion of both the canon and conception of modernism was well underway. However, Ardis's quote indicates the hurdle that scholars faced in broadening both the use and understanding of modernism as a critical idiom. Today, over a decade after its rehabilitation and reevaluation, critics still have not completely altered this popularly held conception of modernism.

Many other critics have even gone one step further than Ardis, suggesting not only that modernists were apolitical but that they in fact reacted against mass culture and the capitalist machinery they believed both produced and encouraged a consumer-oriented culture. Critics have also claimed that these same modernists were largely responsible for the creation of the distinctions between the highbrow and lowbrow in culture, and, indeed, that this bifurcation of the literary marketplace has much to do with the opinions and actions of a number of modernists. Readers might recall the extreme example of literary elitism in Leopold Bloom, the protagonist in James Joyce's

Ulysses, who cleans himself with the papers torn from a popular weekly, epitomizing, as Lawrence Rainey puts it, "the Modernist contempt for popular culture," and, one might add, the commercial aspects of writing (33). "For some scholars," Rainey notes, "that contempt is Modernism's salient characteristic [. . .]. Modernism," he continues, is "a project in which popular culture is construed as a threat of encroaching formlessness, gendered as female, and held at bay by reaffirming and refortifying the boundaries between art and inauthentic mass culture" (34). But, in light of more recent reevaluations of modernism, it could be argued that the term "apolitical" is a misnomer. Social critics such as Pierre Bourdieu have argued quite convincingly that everyone in society is politically and economically engaged, regardless of whether he or she appears reactionary, radical, or indifferent. Furthermore, popular culture is a misleading term because of its fluid nature; what may be considered the avant-garde at one time is popular culture in another place or time. Modernists nonetheless were and still are often described as being "anti-bourgeois"; however, this term, too, is misleading. One must question whether there ever was, or still is, a "bourgeoisie" in the United States. It may have been both dangerous and confusing to attempt to import this most European of terms across the Atlantic.

At the same time that some critics bantered around terms like "anti-bourgeois," the high modernist Henry James criticized American culture for being "classless." This, again, is misleading. Although America may never have had the clear hierarchy and classes that distinguished much of European society, this does not necessarily mean that the United States ever was or is now "classless" and never had its own unique class distinctions. Although these distinctions may not have been, nor are they still, so clearly drawn on birthrights or through business, intellectual, or artistic successes as they were and continue to be in other parts of the world, class distinctions did and still do exist.

But even if "bourgeois" and "class" are eliminated as terms, modernists have also been described as being antagonistic toward "middle-class values." This term too has a dynamic and complex set of parameters and is problematic. The danger in using any of these terms lies in the fact that they seem to indicate a distinct, homogenous, and static group and set of values and therefore lead to even greater confusion in approaching modernist discussions.

For argument's sake, even if a modernist discussion were limited to the original members of the modernist canon and even if it were agreed upon that high modernists were in opposition to the consumer culture around them, inconsistencies in their self-proclaimed apolitical nature are readily apparent. A number of scholars have discussed inconsistencies between the rhetoric and actions of this elite group of writers, identifying instances of these elites' own deliberate participation in the marketplace and consumer culture. Among these "straw men" are Ezra Pound, T. S. Eliot, Virginia Woolf, and various members of the Bloomsbury group. In actual fact, these better-known high modernists as well as many lesser-known and forgotten modernists were active participants in what Bourdieu termed "The Field of Cultural Production." Arguably, modernists' artistic production, concomitant with their active involvement in the consumer culture and free market, is not a divergence from modernism's norm but is, instead, inherent to its nature.

In "The Cultural Economy of Modernism," Lawrence Rainey discusses how a number of high modernists who were presumably antagonistic to the free market, particularly Ezra Pound and T. S. Eliot, often made covert efforts to create an income and wealth through their writing. In the early part of the twentieth century, personal patronage of artists was still actively in practice, but even this patronage was not without its own free market forces. For instance, Margaret Cravens, a wealthy American expatriate, became Pound's patron, allowing him to continue with his largely uncompensated literary work, comforted with the knowledge of a guaranteed income of two hundred pounds per year. To put Pound's yearly allowance in perspective, at the time an industrial worker in England earned approximately seventy-five pounds per year (Rainey 35). Additionally, Rainey highlights Pound's lecture series and other attempts at money-making, such as producing limited editions of publications, despite his constant and simultaneous repudiation of consumer culture, as further examples of Pound's inconsistencies and active participation in the marketplace. In creating an investment-aspect to his books and therefore commodifying what before had only been intellectual property, Pound not only participated, albeit covertly, in the ever-growing mass market but also manipulated the marketplace to his own personal advantage. Pound's theory was that his limited-edition books, like unique pieces of artwork, would go up in value over time because of their inherent scarcity (44–45), a basic tenet of a market-based economy. Rainey argues that the purchasers of these works would also benefit by feeling as though they had moved from the position of mere customers in the marketplace into the elevated realm of art collectors and investors. Rainey describes how Joyce's *Ulysses* was marketed similarly to Pound's limited editions when it appeared in serial form in *The Little Review*—once again a medium with limited circulation that led to an increased inherent economic value resulting from the book's exclusivity and underlying reliance on private patronage. In a similar vein, Eliot chose to have *The Waste Land* published in *Dial* rather than other journals (both prestigious small literary types and larger, more commercial publications) because *Dial* offered two thousand dollars, money he welcomed at the time, and also because the publication was still considered somewhat exclusive in nature and "Eliot wanted his poem to be successful, but not too successful" (51). Rainey adds that Eliot's decision to publish *The Waste Land* in *Dial* was "based on a shrewd assessment of the interaction between aesthetic value, publicity, and money in a market economy" (54).

Throughout his essay Rainey offers clear examples of modernists' understanding and manipulation of the capitalist marketplace and their own seemingly reluctant, yet premeditated and inevitable, participation in the economics of writing. It could, in fact, be said that these high modernists understood the capitalist system more deeply than their commercial contemporaries, the writers of pulp fiction.

Capitalism thrives on supply and demand. Writers of popular or pulp fiction often fill a short-term market niche of "here today, gone tomorrow." The very fact that Pound deliberately set out to create a longer-lasting shelf life for his writing indicates that he understood well the concept of planned obsolescence and the increased economic benefits of long-term investments within a free market economy. Pound and other high modernists distinguished what they were creating from consumer culture by referring to it as "art," even though art is, in fact, consumable. It fulfills a pleasure and need for its public but has, unlike some other consumables, an extended shelf life. With an understanding of this, high modernists also realized that their writing, which may not have been remunerated in the short-term, would possibly achieve greater gains in the long-run. The examples of the royalties that continue for heirs of long-dead writers are numerous. Even the heirs of Mildred Walker continue to benefit from her books' royalties years after her death, as does the literary marketplace in general.

Although Rainey argues that high modernists participated in and at times manipulated the free market to their own advantage, he maintains that they were, in fact, in opposition to the system. In "T. S. Eliot and the Journalistic Struggle," Patrick Collier chips away at this same seemingly implacable high ground of modernism when he adds that it has been "suggested that the success and popularity of mass culture is always a source of repressed envy on the part of modernist elites" (206). Collier further suggests the duplicity of Eliot's feelings when the poet explained the limited success of his own work and that of his contemporaries by "recast[ing] their failure to reach a wide audience as a qualified success—indeed as the only success available to the 'serious man of letters'"(206).

Bonnie Kime Scott approaches this same issue of modernists' avowed detachment from mass culture concomitant with their active participation with it in her discussion of Virginia Woolf, Rebecca West, and Djuna Barnes in "Becoming Professionals." In this essay, she demonstrates these modernist women's participation (at times, both willingly and pleasurably) within the capitalistic mass culture. Of Woolf, she writes that "the origins of her professional persona are harmless enough—a young girl, writing in the comfort of home, mails off her first essay for pay and buys an exotic Persian cat with the proceeds" but then adds that by "1928, Woolf, West, and Barnes all depended upon income for more than their cats—this despite Woolf's famed £500 a year, West's child support from H. G. Wells, and Djuna Barne's occasional checks from Peggy Guggenheim" (209). These changes allow us to study women as producers of a capitalist system" (209).

Scott explains that all these women were "attracted to aristocrats [and that] they took pleasure in beautiful possessions, and interest in their eccentricity, idealized as creative freedom." However, their attraction to the money that came through their families and associations was tempered by their knowledge that "family life could breed financial and emotional interdependencies"—qualities incongruous with the abstract separatist designs of Woolf's and others' work (215). Woolf understood well this danger and proclaimed the necessity of financial independence for a woman—and for any artist—in her famous *A Room of One's Own*.

By 1925 both Woolf and West were writing articles for the profitable and ever-emerging "women's market." Scott writes that when Woolf's contemporary Logan Pearsall Smith criticized her for writing articles for high fees in magazines such as *Vogue* instead of the *Times Literary Supplement* or the *Nation*, Woolf responded with, "I say bunkum. Ladies' clothes and aristocrats playing golf don't affect my style; and they do his a world of good. [. . .] What he [Smith] wants is prestige: what I want, money" (qtd. in Scott, *Refiguring Modernism*: 232).

The alterations in their economic positions and in these authors' reactions in the early decades of the twentieth century further indicate their increased engagement with the market economy. By way of explanation, Rainey concludes his discussion on the economics of modernism by writing, "The Great Depression devastated the fragile economy of Modernism, and in the absence of the patron-investors who had sustained it during the teens and twenties, Modernism turned back to the university, welcoming its direct support" (62). Rainey's statement is inherently limited in its definition of modernism to those writers whom New Critics characterized largely as apolitical or in opposition to mass culture and often members of the Academy. Postmodernism's revision of modernism is far broader than this. However, Rainey's statement merits attention by illustrating the divide between the modernists who were characterized during their own lifetimes as self-made and financially successful in the mass market and those professionally trained writers who often received their opportunities through educational institutions and literary awards and who benefitted from a new and evolving form of "private patronage" derived from "The Academy."

At first glance, Walker appears to belong to this latter category, at least at the commencement of her career. Unlike many modernist writers who began their careers as journalists or copywriters, she decided as a child to someday become a professional novelist and went to college specifically with that goal in mind. Afterward, she sought and found the opportunity to study creative writing in graduate school, a new discipline at that time in the United States. Through this academic association she achieved the start of her professional career as a novelist by receiving the Avery Hopwood Award. This award, a form of "private patronage," not only gave her eleven hundred dollars, a valuable sum in the hard years of the Great Depression and in the early years of her marriage, but it also launched her publishing career with Harcourt Brace (Hugo 62). It should be noted that this new form of private patronage—support from academic institutions—was and arguably still is a typical, if temporary, launching mechanism for new writers. Although it appears that Walker's career as a novelist was nurtured and professionally launched largely through her academic associations, other outside experiences also contributed to her education and career path as a professional writer. Between her undergraduate education and the completion of her master's degree, for example, Walker's first job was as an advertising writer for the John Wanamaker store in Philadelphia (Hugo 51). One of the other modernist novelists who began his career as a copywriter is Sherwood Anderson. No doubt, this work experience in advertising contributed to both authors' understandings of the American marketplace and the utilization of literary tools to engage the public's attention. In Walker's case, this experience may well have augmented the opinions she developed during her undergraduate years at her university. Her work as a retail copywriter would have encouraged this already pragmatic woman to have a greater understanding and acceptance of the necessity for compromise and, moreover, clearly influenced her choice of characters, who were almost always concerned with the economics of survival.

Complicating this early experience with the marketplace, Mildred and Ferdinand Schemm began their married lives and family in the midst of the Great Depression. Certainly, the effects of this economic catastrophe in U.S. culture continued to affect the young novelist's approach to and characterization of American life. Evidence of her own awareness of this compromise, and of the careful distinctions she drew between commercialism and artistic work, is apparent in various comments she made throughout the years and in the actual subject matter of a number of her novels. For instance, the distinction she drew between the fiction of mass culture—the romance novels and sentimental fiction, the novels of "scribbling women"—and serious fiction can be found in a set of file cards she collected over the years from talks she gave. One set of cards recalls her first meeting with Joseph Kinsey Howard, a journalist who became a close friend of the Schemm family. He is best-remembered for his historical account of the development of Montana in *Montana: High, Wide, and Handsome*, published in 1941. After the owner of the Great Falls book store introduced her to Howard, informing him of Walker's latest publication, Howard replied by announcing that he didn't read women's romances. The author promptly corrected him by explaining that *Fireweed* "was a novel about a mill town in the depression." (qtd. in Hugo: 180). Walker's biography also offers other indications of her deliberate distancing from popular fiction. When *The Philadelphia Inquirer* ran a review of *The Curlew's Cry* with the headline "Ranch Girl's Romance," Hugo recalls that her mother's hopes for the novel's success were seared. Hugo further notes "just how resentful Mother could feel about her novels being typed as 'minor,' let alone 'romance'" (185). If Walker had focused only on writing for money, she would have seen these reviews as being positive and helpful because romances usually sold far better than serious fiction.

Walker was not interested in just writing "potboilers" but, like many other modernists, held diffuse and often conflicting goals positioned between a desire to create art and a need to produce an income. Throughout her career, her work's lack of popular acceptance or critical acclaim both confused and disappointed her. In her moments of depression, Walker often seemed to overlook the difficulty of attaining both financial and artistic success simultaneously. Although she was educated and ambitious enough to have read and carefully studied many high modernist writers, she seemed unable at times to differentiate their conception of a novel's success from a popular and financial success in the marketplace.

Walker was by no means alone in this conundrum. Even Ernest Hemingway, so often considered a modernist novelist at the avant-garde and cutting edge of American literature, understood the middle ground he needed to walk in order to develop both as an artist and survive as a novelist. His popular and critical success was unprecedented in American letters. His prose is deceptively simple, sparse, and approachable, and his novels do not seem at all the sort of "grim reading experience" that Richard Poirier believed often characterized the modernist novel (qtd in McGurl: 10). In fact, Hemingway always gave his readers a story, and often the most palatable of stories—the *bildungsroman*. However, despite his popularity among consumers, he was initially categorized alongside the high modernists and still remains one of the most studied and highly regarded modernist writers among critics and scholars today.

In fact, his simultaneous popular and critical success may well be attributed to the fact that he was completely aware of this middle-ground. Throughout his career, Hemingway indicated that he understood and calculated precisely what he intended his fiction to accomplish. Early in his career, as an acknowledgement of his own style, Hemingway commented that his work could be read on two completely different levels, both as a story (a romance, perhaps) and as a poetic work representing something more. With the success of *The Sun Also Rises*, he made his famous "iceberg" comment, indicating that seven-eighths of what was being said was beneath the surface. Hemingway was well aware that his texts operated within two spheres, and he worked seriously and continuously to perfect what he truly saw as his art form, creating a success in the general marketplace and producing "art novels." Through a careful study of literature and the work of his contemporaries, he deliberately attempted to avoid an association in the public's eye with the modernist high ground, even as he simultaneously contributed to what New Critics viewed as high modernism. Even at the end of his career, after the success of *The Old Man and the Sea*,

Hemingway responded (in Spanish) to a question about symbolism—certainly a trademark of his work—"*symbolismo [sic] es un truco nuevo de los intellectuals*" 'symbolism is a new affectation of the intellectuals' (qtd. in Baker, *A Life Story*: 642). Apparently, Hemingway felt that remaining seemingly anti-intellectual was critical to maintaining a partisanship with his readers and the mass market. Hemingway and a number of other modernists were aware that certain traditions of reading were already deeply imbedded in American culture and in readers' expectations of the novel and therefore worked in and around these expectations in the formation of their own styles.

In his subchapter titled "Mental Labor" in *The Rise of the Novel*, Mark McGurl recalls Richard Poirier's account of modernism as "an attempt to perpetuate the power of literature as a privileged form of discourse" in a time of expanding literacy and cultural leveling and his argument that it did so by presenting this relatively new "phenomenon of grim reading," in which reading is less an act of pleasurable consumption than a task of difficult work. Poirier asserted further that modernist literature came to be measured by "the degree of textual intimidation felt in the act of reading," something that could not be easily consumed by what James loathsomely referred to as the "abysmally absorbent" mass consumer culture (qtd. in McGurl: 10–11). However, clearly a number of modernists sidestepped this "grim reading" while simultaneously offering their readers intellectually and ascetically rigorous texts.

This seemingly conflicted position, balancing purpose and style, distinguishes not only Hemingway's work but the prose of many other modernists. Cather's *My Ántonia* and *One of Ours*, for example, are often discussed as examples of her novels that could—and did—receive both popular and critical acclaim. *My Ántonia* can be read on one level as the quintessential celebration of the American dream in the form of the story of a migrant pioneer family that forges a successful life on the American plains. Similarly, *One of Ours* owes its popular success largely to its relevance and readability at the time of its publication, tapping into the general public's need for an inspirational war story. It is the story of a farm boy whose death on the French battlefield in World War I for the cause of freedom can be read as a triumph of the American spirit. However, both these novels have subtexts that are considerably more conflicted and complex. For example, in *My Ántonia*, because of Cather's insertion of an unreliable narrator in the person of Jim Burden, the underlying story becomes more complex than its overriding plot suggests. And *One of Ours*, with its underlying subtext that asks who, exactly, sees the young man's death as heroic, questions popularly held beliefs while simultaneously employing many of the tropes of popular fiction and satisfying the needs of the general reading public. On this subject, Jane Lilienfeld writes, "Willa Cather's novels champion the warrior hero, noble mother-women, the values of hard work, thrift, self-sacrifice, and the American family"—all popular themes in traditional American fiction. She continues, "A less likely modernist would be hard to find. And yet Willa Cather was a master of disguise [. . .]. [Her fiction] defended beauty that shielded hurt, desire, rage and a need to hide" (49).

In the fiction of Hemingway and Cather, readers find clear evidence of both a heightening of the novel's cultural stance in response to the encouragement of James and other high modernists as well as an awareness of popular readers' tastes and the ever-present forces of the American marketplace. Walker's novels also display this careful balancing between economics and aesthetics. This economic-aesthetic tug-of-war, faced by many writers through the ages, particularly exemplifies both the diachronic and synchronic nature of modernism itself. Writing that was caught too much in the moment and concerns of the day or that catered only to those wanting "a light read" might have been popular and profitable, but it was also more likely to become the next day's "mullet wrapper" (being too diachronic). By the same token, fiction written in such a way that it was unapproachable and obscure to most readers was also in danger of molding away in a dusty attic for many years (being too synchronic). Many pragmatic modernists worked to maintain a balance between these two forces.

All evidence points to the fact that Walker wrote to create a lasting piece of literary art and that she took her work and position as an artist extremely seriously; however, her initial artistic inclinations do not diminish the fact that she wrote for money, and that the financial repercussions of her writing were important to her family's livelihood and were ever-present in the back of her mind. Still, Walker maintained detailed journals for each of her novels that include many entries questioning style and the artistic success of the works and that give indications of her aesthetic sensibilities. In her journals she never questioned if a reader would like her work or if it would sell, but her comments were always of an aesthetic nature, such as the following note found in one of her last journals in 1988, concerning her revision of *The Orange Tree*: "The first person won't work for this novel. It's too limiting. There's too much conversation. It seems artificial. Now I'll chuck the twenty odd pages I've changed into first person and go back to third person, but use Tiresa as the 'central consciousness' as H. James calls it" (qtd. in Hugo: 266–67).

Despite these aesthetic inclinations, however, Walker, like Hemingway and Cather, used and often relied upon many of the tropes of sentimental and romantic fiction in the creation of her novels and, one might argue, in the transformation of popular fiction to literary fiction. For instance, one of the most persistent tropes of sentimental fiction is the marriage plot, which Walker utilizes in a number of her novels.

A closer examination of *The Curlew's Cry* reveals Walker implementing and altering the tropes of sentimental fiction. Early in the novel, when Pamela loses her chances with the man she hopes to marry, her mother practically orchestrates an alternate marriage between Pamela and the son of a wealthy business associate. Pamela, like so many heroines in sentimental novels of the past, marries for reasons other than love. The narrative points out that although Pamela's husband is no rake, his father's involvement with the economic demise of her family's cattle ranch implicates him and somehow cheapens the marriage. Despite Pamela's extended residence outside of Montana in New York, the kindness of her husband, and the strong overtures by both her mother and mother-in-law for grandchildren, Pamela remains childless and eventually leaves New York. Although she does not return to her hometown ill, with a child, or near death, the price that she must pay for her deviation from the expected social norms is a lonely life as an outcast divorcée. By portraying the tribulations of a "fallen woman," Walker seems to be following the course of the traditional sentimental novel. However, at this point, she also complicates the narrative of the sentimental novel. Pamela's original desire for her childhood beau and friend, Wrenn Morley, remains intact, even though he is married to her best friend and they have been apart for so many years. Because of her infatuation with Morley, Pamela remains vulnerable, and because of her emotional vulnerability, readers familiar with the tropes of sentimental fiction are again willing to accept this seemingly uncharacteristic quality in the novel's heroine. However, in a departure from the tropes of sentimental fiction, after a number of years living alone back in Montana and during her private success as a businesswoman, Pamela is eventually overwhelmed with the revelation that her passion for Wrenn is and perhaps only ever was a distracting piece of whimsy, imagined wholly on her part. At this point in the novel, Pamela realizes that she has incorrectly attributed all her real frustrations to this seemingly unrequited passion with Morley, avoiding the true issues in her life. Pamela comes to understand that her actual desire has always been for her own independence and her close relationship with the land and a few good friends. Here, the novelist has departed truly from the tropes of the sentimental novel. Interestingly, Pamela's revelation does not emerge explicitly in the novel, and no guiding narrator explains exactly what it is that Pamela eventually comes to understand and feel; instead, a reader must discover these revelations from what is written between the lines, or within the "vacuoles," and within the novel's subtle symbolism. In *The Curlew's Cry*, Walker layers her version of the sentimental novel with these deviations from predictable tropes, and the novel is just one example of how Walker, like so many other modernists, was able to write for a market demanding "a good read" while also developing more complex ideas. As was the case with so many other modernists, she walked in that middle ground, and in doing so contributed to a unique form of modernism.

Furthermore, Walker did not try to be apolitical or overlook the tenuous and often fragile hold that the American middle class had on their own finances and future. In fact, both her own life and the lives of her characters were caught in this middle-class struggle. Throughout her life and career she neither wholeheartedly celebrated the consumer culture nor completely denigrated the capitalist system. As in all matters, she held an ambiguous middle ground, constantly exploring and interacting with the vicissitudes of the U.S. marketplace.

Another example of the balance Walker maintained between her art and the marketplace can be found in the self-sketch (both factual and promotional) written for an introduction to the condensed version of *Winter Wheat* that appeared in the December 1943 issue of *Ladies' Home Journal*. Ripley Hugo notes how her mother both announces her accomplishments and amusedly "downplays her successes" and, in doing so, creates a marketable literary persona:

> Somehow, in between the hilarious and strenuous business of living, five novels—*Winter Wheat*, Literary Guild Selection for February, published by Harcourt Brace & Co., is the sixth—found their stubborn ways between covers. I'd rather write them than struggle with fall canning, and I like to think they are as important as canning, but on a cold

> winter's day I would want the other members of the family to vote on it. (qtd. in Hugo: 149)

Walker's comments here offer evidence that she, like Hemingway and other modernist writers, understood and encouraged the promotional value of her own down to earth personality alongside her fiction.

Walker's earlier fiction indicates an optimism about free enterprise that she may have also felt personally in those years, despite the Depression. However, as time passed and her readership tapered off, she became increasingly critical of consumer culture. For instance, the fascination Julia Hauser has in all the new products she sees at the Philadelphia Exposition of 1876 in one of Walker's early novels, *Light from Arcturus*, is in stark contrast to the tone of the author's later journal entries and novels on this same subject. The characters in her last novel, *The Orange Tree*, frequently question how a culture can cheapen the meaning of a sacred word like "joy" by using it to name everything from a cookbook to a sex manual to a dish detergent. Also, in a journal entry written after her return to the United States following a year abroad, when she taught as a Fulbright scholar in war-torn Japan, Walker gives further evidence of her attenuated feelings on American consumerism. As she travels back home, she writes: "The luxury of this train offends me [. . .]. Japan grows on me as I get further away. [. . .] I don't mean to be dramatic and perhaps I am under the influence of a kind of nostalgia for Japan and the Ugly A. [reading *The Ugly American*] [. . .]. I'm going to impose new standards of personal frugality [. . .]" (qtd. in Hugo: 233).

Karl Marx characterized the capitalistic system by its necessity for "creation and recreative destruction, renewal, innovation and constant change [which] are also the dynamics of Modernism" (qtd. in Childs: 32). In *All That Is Solid Melts Into Air*, Marshall Berman argues strongly for the connection between Marxist criticism and modernism. Whether the free market system is cast or interpreted in a positive or negative light, Walker's novels repeatedly fictionalize capitalism's economic dynamism and its effects upon her characters and in this way are in accordance with Berman's theories. For instance, the crisis that fuels the underlying tension in her first novel, *Fireweed*, is economically driven. First, the novel's characters must survive as underpaid mill workers and lumbermen in a dying company town. Then, the entire country faces a cataclysmic economic depression. From start to finish this first novel, completed during the Great Depression, focuses on family finances and economic survival. However, despite its subject matter, the novel neither denigrates capitalism nor characterizes the economic upheavals as entirely negative. In fact, in *Fireweed* capitalism feeds upon its own crises, as Marx hypothesized. The mill's departure from the town forces Celie and her husband to reevaluate their own situation. The exodus of out-of-town money creates a small economic niche in which this young family discovers its future. This economic scenario is freer and potentially more lucrative than its predecessor and is an example of Marx's belief in capitalism's re-creative destruction and renewal.

Again, capitalism's upheavals and re-creations are apparent in *The Brewers' Big Horses* and *The Curlew's Cry*. In both these novels, the economic collapses of ways of doing business create new opportunities for the novels' characters. When, in *The Brewers' Big Horses*, Prohibition is legalized, Sara must find an alternative source of business for the family brewery. As a result, she creates a "beer-less beer garden" and ultimately contributes to the vertical diversification of the U.S. beer industry. Similarly, in *The Curlew's Cry*, when the era of the maverick rancher comes to an end in Montana, Pamela picks up the pieces of her father's bankrupt cattle ranch and successfully pioneers the dude ranch industry in the West. These characters are by-products of the U.S. economic system and attempt to work within this system to advance their own best interests and the interests of those around them. Out of the destruction of one system, these characters contribute to the creation of its successor.

Perhaps Walker's deepest reflection and most pessimistic questioning of the intersection and occasional disparity between personal success and public service within the U.S. marketplace can be found in her novel *Medical Meeting*. In this novel, Dr. Henry Baker and his wife, Liz, are presented as a husband and wife team who sacrifice twelve years of their lives working in solitude, relative poverty, and obscurity in an attempt to find a cure for tuberculosis. When they finally have a breakthrough and discover a mold, microcydin, which after twenty-five test cases clears the tuberculin lungs, they are invited to a medical conference in Chicago to present their findings. However, their discovery is upstaged by a paper presented the day before their own, demonstrating a more effective and reliable cure for the same disease. Henry and Liz are devastated, and this crisis precipitates a series of questions and misgivings in both of them concerning their seemingly altruistic ambitions and the entire system within which they operate. When faced with this failure, the Bakers begin to question their personal motivations. They reflect and consider that, for all those years, they claimed that all they wanted was to help humanity and be like the Curies. However, their current crisis forces them to question why they should not now be pleased that someone else has finally found a cure for this horrible disease and also to wonder how much of their work had been motivated by their own egos. As Dr. Baker and Liz delve into this matter they are also aware that the group that succeeded was, in fact, a well-funded, large, and legitimate group of individuals working within an official institution. Realizing this, the Henrys again must ask themselves how they possibly could have been so deluded to think that they, working alone and without institutional funding, could have expected to perform something akin to a miracle. Underlying this question is a subtextual interrogation of one commonly held tenet of America's entrepreneurial philosophy: the belief that each individual, acting in his or her own best interest, will ultimately find a niche and fulfill the greater needs of society at large.

Their confidence shaken, if not destroyed, the Bakers can only wonder how their actions, based on what they had originally perceived as foundational U.S. values, could have deceived and led them to their current failure.

In one passage, the narrator writes of Henry, "There was one thing, though, that he wanted to get straight with Paul [a medical colleague]—that part of the identification with the myth. If he and Liz had ever had any idea that they were like the Curies because of the similarity between their difficulties and drudgery and sacrifices, they had no such idea now" (198). Readers must wonder what Henry means when he thinks of "the identification with the myth." "Myth" could refer to his belief that two individuals could possibly re-create a miracle similar to the Curies', or it could refer to the "myth" of creation or the "myth" of the American dream—of the belief that a diligent, independent, and single-minded enterprise is ultimately rewarded. In fact, the use of the word "myth" here could refer to all these concepts.

When the Bakers return home, in a moment of despair, Liz angrily dumps all their research material out into the yard and disinfects the laboratory. Liz performs this act of sabotage because she wants to create closure for this chapter of their lives. She wants her husband to put his research interests behind him and take a more traditional and better-paying job as a full-time doctor in a hospital. Throughout the novel a tension underlies the sacrifices Liz and her daughter have made for Henry's dream, such as living in a small rental cottage and doing without—all for the sake of science. Even when Liz attends the medical conference and reunites with the other wives whom she knew from Henry's medical school days, she is ashamed and frustrated that she has to borrow a dress for the affair from a wealthier friend and also has to worry over the price of a hotel sandwich. However, at the end of the novel, when Henry finally recapitulates and accepts the sabotage of his research and commences with the superintendent's job at the sanitarium, despite the raise in income, status, and the luxury of a large, well-furnished home that result from this, Liz is still overwhelmed with misgivings. As she navigates through the politics of her first meal with the sanitarium board members, she considers how mundane a successful middle-class life will be in comparison to the destitute but highly intellectually charged life of a researcher. As Liz considers all these things, the group's dessert is interrupted when Dr. Baker receives a phone call. At this point in the novel, his research colleague offers him a research posting and needs an immediate response. As Henry stands alone in the cold pantry, he considers the options, pondering his chances to continue his research, and thinks to himself that "[h]e would have no safe berth, no capital. There would be no security [. . .] except the security in his own mind" (276). At this same point in the novel, unknown to Henry Baker, his wife's thoughts in the other room almost mirror his own.

Throughout *Medical Meeting*, both characters seem to resent the force that a consumer culture has over them. In their own ways, the Bakers are both reflective and representative of the experimental modernists, motivated by illusive goals that could not be measured and simultaneously frustrated by their exclusion from the economic success of others around them. Although the novel ends with Henry accepting the better-paying job and more secure institutional position and, in fact, with the Bakers fulfilling the "traditional American dream," its conclusion is open-ended and indicates that the Bakers' decision may well be temporary. *Medical Meeting* ends with a metaphorical scene. When a board member offers Liz a seat in an expensive Savonarola chair, Liz politely accepts, saying, "It's an interesting chair, isn't it? But I wouldn't want to settle down in it for any length of time" (280). This final comment in *Medical Meeting* might be interpreted as an example of Walker's modernist high ground. Certainly, Liz's comment appears anti-commercial, implying the superiority of intellectual and experimental life over a comfortable, consumer-oriented, middle-class existence.

However, Mark McGurl, in *The Novel Art*, offers another way of interpreting scenes such as this one. McGurl argues that readers must reinterpret Marxist criticism in light of the changes in the world economy in the last fifty years. McGurl writes: "Despite its [modernism's] frequently antibourgeois rhetoric, the emergence of the art-novel in the United States must be situated within—without simply being collapsed into—the much larger context of the expansion of the 'new middle' or 'professional managerial' class in the late-nineteenth and early-twentieth centuries." (11) Identified chiefly by intellectual or mental work they performed, this emergent "new middle / managerial" class formation suggests a significant transformation from Marx's "laboring class" of the nineteenth-century. In his study, McGurl explains that as the twentieth century progressed, a greater percentage of the middle class began to work with people and ideas rather than with raw materials and manufactured items. This transformation of the middle class continues today. Members of the middle class are no longer solely manual laborers but are, increasingly, "intellectual laborers" (11). McGurl argues, moreover, that the subject matter and form of the American novel reflect this evolution in America's middle class. Victorian novels emphasized morality, with its heroes often rewarded for their "good choices." Novels that followed the Victorian works—and the evolution of their readers—emphasized intellectual vigor; in other words, "intelligence" rather than "virtue" was rewarded. Throughout Walker's novels, there are numerous examples of this intellectual work. Repeatedly, after careful and individual thought, her novels' characters solve their dilemmas and their "intellectual vigor" is rewarded. Read in this light, even Walker's later fiction appears less "anti-bourgeois"—or anti-commercial—than it might have otherwise. If read with McGurl's suggestion in mind, her fiction, and *Medical Meeting* in particular, celebrates the newly emerging American middle class with its "intellectual laborers" and their concerns over intellectual property rights and issues of remuneration for ideas and mental prowess.

Accepting McGurl's argument that intellectual laborers are America's new middle class and reading Walker's fiction in this light, her participation in the American marketplace and pragmatism appear anything but apolitical. In fact, her form of modernism can be viewed as both proactive and sympathetic to the newly emerging and ever-evolving American middle class. The same can also be said for many other modernist writers who sensed, if only intuitively, that the composition of the American middle class was changing from manual to mental laborers as western culture evolved from an age of industrialism to an age of information and technology.

5. Mildred Walker's Wars

Mildred Walker's mother, Harriet Merrifield, was born in 1865 to church bells tolling for the death of Abraham Lincoln. Mildred's father was born in 1862, during the height of the American Civil War. The future writer's early childhood was no doubt colored by stories of this war told by friends, family, and elderly veterans in their sixties and seventies, sharing their memories from the peaceful summer porches of their Vermont homes. Despite the quiet comportment of the veterans, their messages must have rung clearly in that young girl's ears, warning her that peace was, at best, tenuous.

Coincidentally, the year of Walker's birth was marked by the release of Albert Einstein's four papers detailing his special theory of relativity, the relationships between mass and energy, the Brownian theory of motion, and another theory formulating the photon theory of light—papers that would eventually change the course of human history. In the years to follow, an adolescent Walker walked with soldiers in the busy Philadelphia streets, overhearing news and stories of the First World War. She was twelve, an impressionable age, when the United States entered World War I. The reality and images she carried with her of World War I, "the war to end all wars," grew even more vivid with her marriage to a veteran of that war. Ferdinand Schemm returned from World War I and went on to practice medicine. Although Dr. Schemm wanted to serve directly in World War II, previous injuries and a shortage of medical practitioners in Montana prevented his reenlistment in the U.S. military (Hugo 99). Despite this and the family's seemingly quiet life in the safely remote western town of Great Falls, Montana, they too were drawn into this international conflict. Remembering these war years, the novelist's daughter, Ripley Hugo, writes:

> George and I remember the war years from that [Great Falls] house. We had blackout curtains, sugar coupons, gasoline coupons. We were trained as bicycle couriers; our fleet was stationed at the nearby hospital to carry messages in case phone connections should be severed. We were also taught to recognize the smells of poisonous gases. When we went to the movies, we learned the propaganda of the war effort. [. . .]
>
> In those days Great Falls lived in the shadow of the newly built East Air Force Base. The base was the last stop for "lend-lease" planes being flown to Russia when that country became one of the Allies. There were Russian pilots in the town and, often, Russian interpreters. (100)

After World War II, this same Great Falls base continued to be a military base, serving as a strategic site during the Cold War. The family's involvement with the military did not end with World War II. Ferdinand and Mildred Walker Schemm sent their eldest teenage son, George, off to a military preparatory school, and their younger son, Christopher, eventually served the U.S. government for many years as a surgeon in the military. The Schemms' daughter, Ripley, married David Hansen in 1952, only to separate from him months later with his departure for training and military service in the Korean conflict.

During her years of teaching in Aurora between 1955 and 1968, Walker, rarely without a copy of the Sunday edition of the *New York Times*, read accounts of Martin Luther King Jr.'s campaigns against racial segregation in the south, the 1961 Bay of Pigs Invasion, President John F. Kennedy's assassination in 1963, and Israel's Six-Day War and occupation of the Gaza Strip in 1967. She also witnessed the increasingly heated civilian demonstrations against U.S. involvement in the Vietnam conflict. In fact, in her mother's biography, Hugo notes that even in 1970, when she had been invited back to Wells College to give a speech, the event was cancelled because "the students called a [war] strike [. . .]" (250).

The *Times*, along with television and radio newscasts, also brought the elderly author news of Ayatollah Khomeini and his followers overthrowing the Shah of Iran in 1979, of outbreaks of AIDS in 1981, of the Falkland War in 1982, and of the Salvadorian and Nicaraguan conflicts in 1982 and 1983. The year before her novels began appearing again in print, and four years before her death, she heard news of the Allied forces, headed by President George H. W. Bush, launching Desert Storm on January 15, 1991.

The author was by no means alone in witnessing these events, but she offered a singular rendering of them in her novels. These novels demonstrate her keen powers of observation, fictional prowess, and her sense of personal involvement in world events. Furthermore, her use of fiction as a legitimate forum for this discourse again demonstrates her belief in literature as a critical and acceptable means of interaction and involvement with her society and the events of the day. Given the positive public response her novels received, she was not alone in this belief. For instance, in *Writing for Her Life*, Ripley Hugo discusses some of the letters, housed in the archives of the University of Wyoming, that her mother received from readers concerning *Winter Wheat*. Because this was one of the first American novels to be printed in a paperback edition for distribution overseas to the armed forces, Walker received a number of these letters from soldiers stationed in Europe. One, sent by Sergeant Edward Urbanich, dated December 20, 1944, reads:

> I wonder if when you wrote *Winter Wheat*, you realized that it would be read by one of America's soldiers in far-off Belgium? I picked the book out of the [Special Services]

> collection mainly because of the title; I almost knew those two words meant home. They did, too, for I call Montana—Great Falls, to be exact—my home. Although I am not too familiar with wheat farming, I have associated with enough folks at home to know that you have captured all that is in what might be termed Montana's greatest contribution to the world. I have felt the life at home even more vividly than memories can bring, just by reading your magnificent novel. [. . .] I can appreciate your comparison of wheat and life—it was very good. Somehow, I had never stopped to think about it. [. . .] I like the thought so much that I know I shall think of it many times in the future. (146)

It is evident here that Sgt. Edward Urbanich saw his reasons for fighting captured in Walker's novel. Although he does not comment on the novel's discussion of the war itself, he seems aware of the timeliness and relevance of the text to himself and other soldiers. *Winter Wheat* by no means sentimentalized the American middle-class life that soldiers such as Urbanich hoped to return to; instead, it is a story of struggle. Still, the hardscrabble existence in the dry plains of Montana was a struggle that many soldiers were happy to turn their thoughts toward and was one that soldiers such as Urbanich claimed they could understand, perhaps unlike their current endeavors. Moreover, Urbanich's letter also gives evidence of the globalization of his perspective when he writes, "Montana's greatest contribution to the world." Having now experienced life across the Atlantic, he no longer views Montana as a singular landscape but as part of a global community.

Many of the military events of the twentieth century as well as Walker's personal experiences with the wars that affected her can be found both embedded and sometimes openly discussed in much of her fiction. For instance, in *If a Lion Could Talk*, a historical novel spanning the years prior to the outbreak of the Civil War, Mark Ryegate, a Baptist minister from a quiet Massachusetts town, joins John Brown's movement. Walker began writing the novel in the 1960s and witnessed its publication in the 1970s, a time when the United States was still very much in the grips of the Vietnam conflict. One of the timely issues addressed in this novel is the true motivation behind Mark Ryegate's participation in the Abolitionist movement. Readers learn that although the antislavery cause is important to Mark Ryegate, his wife, Harriet, astutely notes that her husband's fervor for participation in this cause comes shortly after his failed efforts at missionary work among the Montana natives. With his announcement to join John Brown's cause in Kansas, Harriet responds by saying: "And this time I can't follow you. [. . .] When you went to the Wilderness [in what is now Montana] I didn't know any better. Now you have a new lure" (185). "Lure" appears to be a strange way to describe participation in the abolitionist cause, but Harriet senses that her husband, now floundering in his own faith and sense of purpose, is a prime candidate to be "lured" by someone else's cause and that, no matter how worthy the cause, there is inherently an insincerity and weakness in a man who runs from what he cannot understand to fight in someone else's battle. As their conversation becomes more heated, Harriet adds, "I've just been stupid not to see before. You've deceived yourself, just as you did about your call to the missionary field. You went out to the Wilderness—to use it, because you thought preaching to Indians would make you more eloquent. 'Lure' was the right word" (186). Later, when Mark is alone and muses over his wife's words, he thinks to himself, "That's what Harriet thinks. She sees my joining the movement and going to Kansas as a cause to lose myself in. A lure. A cause and a lure are worlds apart. Is there anything wrong with a cause?" (207). Mark tries to convince himself of his sincerity as he embarks on his next quest. At the conclusion of the novel and upon Mark's return, injured and much the wiser, he thinks, "What a posturing, yapping, humorless fool he had been, lost in the forest of his own trite verbiage" (273).

Reading these comments, it is not difficult to see the connection between the Ryegates' skepticism of the individual sincerity and motivation of those participating in "movements" and the questions that many U.S. citizens in the 1970s must have had when they witnessed the many individuals caught up in movements of one type or another, like peace protests or women's rallies. Although Walker carefully avoided a direct discussion of the issues of the day, she nonetheless implicitly explored her thoughts, and those of her readers, concerning the sincerity and motivation behind some individuals' participation in the protest movements during the 1960s and '70s.

Furthermore, Walker addresses the differences between combatants' and noncombatants' perspectives on war in a number of her novels. In *The Quarry*, the novel's protagonist, Lyman Converse, lives long enough to witness both his brother leaving to be a soldier in the Civil War and his son enlisting in World War I. At the start of the novel, Lyman is too young to enlist in the Civil War and even tries to run off and join against his parents' wishes. Through Lyman's boyish daydreams, Walker focuses the narrative on the dangerous romanticism that some young men attached to their enlistment:

> June 10, 1864
>
> He thought about the uniform he would have, like Dan's [his older brother's]. He had tried on Dan's cap with the green fir-tree insignia of Vermont on it. He handled Dan's gun and felt the edge of the bayonet. Maybe Louisa would make him a housewife mending kit to carry as she had John, with his name embroidered on it. [. . .] Maybe he would be mentioned in the dispatch for bravery and [. . .]. (75–76)

In this daydream, readers get a glimpse of Lyman's hero fantasy of being recognized by his brother, his town, and his secret sweetheart. Walker comments that "[i]f he were killed, he'd have seen some fighting anyway," a reflection of Lyman believing that in battle he would at least have died a man—and not the boy he is—and that somehow, seeing and participating in death is the simplest and most direct path to manhood (76).

When he tries and fails to forge his father's name for permission to join the army under the legal age, Lyman sells the family's old cart horse to the military so he might feel as though he has contributed to the war effort. However, when his father discovers this, he is furious, and Lyman belatedly realizes his own mistake. Throughout the novel, Lyman is portrayed as an outsider. Somehow, he senses that if he had been given an opportunity to fight, his transition into manhood would have been simpler and more natural, and he would no longer feel like a mere observer to the life around him. He is haunted by the belief that to truly live, a man should fight. As *The Quarry* closes and Lyman's only son goes off to join up in World War I, Lyman once again feels an outsider. His son is almost a throwback to his elder brother: mysterious, brave, and male. When a neighbor asks Lyman about his son's enlisting, he responds by saying, "I don't know [. . .]. But he's twenty-five, he's not a boy any more. I guess he knows more than we do about what's going on over there." To which Mr. Peterboro responds, "Brings it kinda close to home, don't it?" (339). Certainly for Lyman, the comment carries a deeper import than the speaker had intended.

Clearly, one of the issues addressed in this historical novel is the role of combatants and noncombatants in wartime, especially how noncombatant men devalue themselves during wartime. This is an issue that would have been relevant not only to readers in 1947, when *The Quarry* was published, but also to the Schemm family in those war years while the novel was written, particularly given the fact that Walker's husband wanted to fight in World War II but was unable to do so (Hugo 99). This is not to suggest that Dr. Schemm suffered as Lyman Converse did, but instead, to note the fact that the subject would have had some personal relevance to the family.

In *The Brewers' Big Horses*, Walker again approaches war's repercussions on the home front and on noncombatants when the novel's protagonist, Sara Bolster, receives her own form of shell shock after residents of the town demonstrate their deep-seated prejudices and turn publicly against her husband's German-American family and friends during the outbreak of World War I, despite the fact that her family was one of the first members of this Midwestern town. When Sara Bolster's sister-in-law, Ottilie Henkel, is snubbed by the Women's Century Club, the author utilizes the scene to demonstrate the pains of war inflicted upon noncombatants. As one of the sisters, Marie, idly remarks, "It was so lovely along the drive this afternoon, it didn't seem as though that terrible war [World War I] could be going on over there," Ottilie is still stinging from the hurt the snubbing has caused her and announces, "The war is going on over here, too!" And then, when Sara later asks her sisters-in-law why the women's group has not accepted Ottilie's piece of artwork for exhibition, she is told: "My dear Sara, the name is too German. The committee seems to feel it would be unwise to have it made by a Hun." Marie adds, "It's a pity, though. Father came to this country as a boy. He was proud of his citizenship. Uncle Hans fought in the Civil War. Now we must be insulted because our name happens to be German!" (355–56).

No doubt, Walker was all too aware of the prejudices erroneously attached to ethnic groups in times of war, having herself married into a German-American family. This narrative clearly is sympathetic to these ethnic groups and can be read as the author's own active participation in the discourse of war—war on the home front.

The author's interest in "noncombatants' wars" is again addressed in *The Curlew's Cry*. In this novel, Wrenn Morley returns from military service, never having "seen action," to his hometown of Brandon Rapids, Montana, in 1918, only to discover the devastation and horrors of the Spanish influenza, an event inextricably tied to that war. In an interesting revision of the traditional war novel, when Wrenn Morley returns from the military in *The Curlew's Cry*, Walker clearly portrays Pamela Lacey as the combatant. Morley arrives to find his daughter dead and

Pamela exhausted from nursing his wife. Despite Pamela's exhaustion, it is Morley—the male soldier—who is the weaker of the two. "The khaki uniform made Wrenn's face colorless" (294), Pamela notices. Throughout the novel, Wrenn has been Pamela's great conjure, a man whom she imagines to be strong and whom she thinks she wants and needs. Upon his return from the military, however, when a reader might expect him to look his most distinguished and masculine, he falls far short of Pamela's expectations. It is in this moment that Pamela realizes that she does not love him and Walker "puts on its head" the traditional love story of the woman waiting for her man to return from war. Here, the man returning from the military is something less than Pamela envisioned, and instead of being embraced in his strong fighting arms—as is the case in many sentimental novels—she flees from them.

Again, in *Unless the Wind Turns*, Walker makes the connection between events far from the battlefront war and issues directly connected to war. In this novel, while eastern tourists wander on an ill-fated pack trip on the slopes of the Rocky Mountains, debating the pros and cons of the U.S. involvement in World War II, they are engulfed in a forest fire that they never believed could touch them. With this as the external drama, the novel subtextually explores issues concerning America's entry into World War II. As Lizzie and Serena lay out under the stars, camping and worrying about their husbands battling the forest fire, they allow their minds to wander. Their conversation reveals the issues surrounding the war and women's perceptions of their roles in both the war and war discourse. This dialogue begins with a description of the fire-lit sky, metaphoric of the spread of conflict around the globe:

> The entire sweep of sky from the dark rim of low mountain reef across to the snow-topped peak was colored red.
>
> "It's [the fire's] gone way around the edge!" Lizzie whispered so as not to wake Rose. "They'll never get it stopped."

> "You're right, Lizzie, about this seeming like a war," Serena murmured. "You know, you read about those truck-loads of soldiers going through those towns in Europe all night, moving up to the front line. I suppose women lie in bed and count the trucks and wait the way we've been doing. Sometimes, I'd give anything to be over there helping some way."
>
> "Oh, Serena, you're crazy. We're lucky to be here," Lizzie said softly. "Why, you sound like a child craving excitement." (127)

At this point in the text, the women continue to debate their involvement in the war. Serena tries to explain to Lizzie how she would like to be involved in the actual conflict, but Lizzie argues that their war work at home is more than just busy work. However, Serena, the more independent of the two women, concludes with: "'Women in England and Europe, even in Germany, lots of them, must know they're living as people never lived before; they must know what they believe in or don't believe in, no matter what they're suffering or doing without or what they've lost. We don't. All the war means to us is heavier taxes.'" (128) Because both Lizzie and Serena express valid viewpoints, readers get a sense of the author's own reluctance to voice any one opinion on this war but still recognize her active desire to engage and explore the issues and debates surrounding the conflict. Each character's thoughts are expressed with equal clarity, and the narrative does not favor one opinion over the other. In Lizzie, readers sense what might be considered the more stereotypical feminine voice, the voice favoring a safe distance from danger and an acceptance of her peripheral role in the war effort. In Serena, readers get a taste of what might be viewed as the more modern, aggressive, and questioning feminine voice. This voice questions the value of her distanced, noncombatant role in the war efforts. During the war, Walker did engage in the same efforts that Serena refers to as "busy work." No doubt, as she participated in fundraisers and other war efforts, the author herself must have at times had second-thoughts about the value of these supportive roles relative to the contributions of combatants.

Issues surrounding World War II also emerge through the debates held by the other characters in *Unless the Wind Turns*. For example, one character, Victor, is a refugee from the First World War with a past that is somewhat murky, but the other characters in the novel do know that he escaped from Austro-Hungary and "the *Aunschluss* people" (35). Prior to this trip, Serena has played an active roll in helping this intellectual secure an apartment and speaking engagements in the United States and has thoughtfully included him in their family holiday. At the start of the trip, Serena enjoys Victor's cool rationalism and intellectualism. However, this changes when the forest fire breaks out. As the rest of the men are trapped in the woods while searching for a wood cutter, Victor emerges from the bush and joins the women and is then asked why he didn't stay and try to help find the lost man. He explains, "Because I couldn't see the point of inexperienced men like Walt and myself, even John, going in on that trip [to save the wood cutter from the fire]. You Americans rush after danger rather eagerly, you know" (165). Victor then adds that he is sure that the wood cutter is most likely dead anyway and says, "You see what I mean? You're used to reading about horror and death and war, not to facing it. That makes the difference. I simply state the probable facts, and you think me heartless [. . .]" (165). Although Victor is in fact right—the young man has already burnt to death—Serena's opinion of Victor changes radically during his explanation. Although he continues on, as he always has, talking about "realistic European psychology," Serena, who herself had been previously detached from the plight of the people around her, can now only think of the young man's wife preparing to give birth to their child while her husband burns to death. At this point, Serena has no time for Victor's pontificating, and he shifts in her estimation from a worldly, knowledgeable man to a selfish coward. Walker writes, "At this moment [Victor's talk] seemed shallow and heartless. She was impatient to be on her way" (166).

Many Americans must have debated U.S. involvement in the war effort as the characters in this novel do, especially prior to the bombing of Pearl Harbor. In the novel, Serena suddenly decides that there has been enough talk and reasoning—that people are destroyed each day in war's conflagrations and that caring human beings should simply jump in after them. The crisis of the fire brings Serena to a greater sense of responsibility and sympathy with humanity. *Unless the Wind Turns* was released in 1941, the same year the Japanese attacked Pearl Harbor. To today's readers, the planes buzzing overhead to fight the Montana fires in the novel are ominously reminiscent of the droning of planes over the Hawaiian Islands. With the unexpected fire forcing her characters' into personal involvement, Walker presciently created an analogy for Pearl Harbor's effect on Americans' involvement in the war.

The definition of war fiction and the relationship between the world wars and the modernist sensibility have been, and continue to be, contentious issues. Furthermore, the role that women and noncombatants had in this and other wars is still a source of lively debate, as are the distinctions critics have traditionally made between combatant and noncombatant literature, the war front and the home front, and the private versus public renderings of war. In most of these discussions, World War I, "the war to end all wars," is still the most common point of departure for modernist discussions, particularly in discussions of high modernism. Peter Childs sums up the relevance of World War I to modernist thought with the following:

> World War I and the years immediately before and after it, brought about the demise of many institutions and beliefs; the class system [in England] was rocked by the rise of trade unions and the Labour party; beliefs in King and Country; patriotism and duty were betrayed by the carnage of war; the strength of the patriarchy was challenged as women went to work outside the home and the suffrage movement gained hold. In terms of trauma itself, the effect

> on modern consciousness cannot be overstated. [. . .] The war produced a deep distrust of optimistic secular or teleological understandings of history and seemed a climactic, severing event that showed conclusively the failures of nineteenth-century rationalism. (20)

With a heightened awareness of social inequities, vivid images of war, the collapse of entire social systems, and the inevitable erosion of firmly held ideals, it is no wonder that fiction emerging from this period often portrayed life negatively. In her introductory paragraph to "The Question of Modernism" in *The American Novel, 1914–1945*, Linda Wagner-Martin writes that modernism "was startling in its innovation and dramatic in its concision, as it spoke for a 'wasteland' view of existence" (1). Wagner-Martin characterizes modern writing as "also almost completely, sometimes overwhelmingly serious," stricken by "the ultimate recognition—the meaninglessness of human life" (6). Although some writers did present the "traditional war story" with very serious and negative portrayals of the frontline and details of specific military actions, Wagner-Martin cites a number of instances in early war writing in which authors tended to miniaturize the war and instead focused on the lives of selected soldiers. She notes further that the line between journalism, with its concrete and factual reporting, and modernist fiction, influenced by writers such as Hemingway and Martha Gellhorn, became increasingly blurred. Novels, Wagner-Martin writes, were less anti-enemy and more often discussions from a philosophical perspective with humane questions about repression, fascism, and killing. The individual prowess and courage marking many early war novels became less of a focal point as fiction "stressed group identification over the earlier romantic idealism" (129). Wagner-Martin points out that modernism's approach to the topic of war evolved and that even Hemingway's *For Whom the Bell Tolls* appeared strangely out of place alongside his earlier war fiction, which epitomizes the individual man's "grace under pressure" and valorizes individual bravery, by instead presenting "the image of the bell tolling [as] the signal of human brotherhood" (130). Although Wagner-Martin's comment rightly locates an emphasis on brotherhood in *For Whom the Bell Tolls*, it merits closer scrutiny. Presumably Wagner-Martin is referring to Hemingway's seminal war novel *A Farewell to Arms* when she refers to "his earlier war fiction." However, a closer examination reveals that, even in this novel, much of the war is fought far from the battlefield, in a hospital bed, a somewhat domestic setting.

Wagner-Martin also notes that the dark tones of war fiction carried over into other subjects in the writing of the 1930s and 1940s and cites the impact of Albert Camus' *L'Étranger*, which reinforced the public's sense that modern life had become increasingly inhumane and that the brutality of war was only mirroring many of life's other disappointments (130). However, in some of her final remarks on the subject of the world wars and modernist fiction, Wagner-Martin adds, "Other books published between 1940 and 1945 were studiedly reflective, not denying all hope but trying to find new answers to eternal questions" (130). The novels of Walker may be categorized in this last group.

Certainly, Walker's fiction written during these years may be described as "serious and studiedly reflective" but also may be characterized as forever searching for "new answers to eternal questions"—questions about love, loyalty, and the meaning of family, community, and success. Her fiction was neither without hope nor solely focused on man's destructive inhumanity. To characterize or define what actually constitutes war literature and to highlight the distinctions critics and the public have drawn historically between combatant and noncombatant literature and male and female war literature, Bonnie Kime Scott asks, "How did the Great War, which has generally been seen as a deep influence on modernist views of the world, have different effects on men and women writers?" (5) Scott then answers this question: "Men who went to the front, some experiencing injury and death, such as Rupert Brooke, Siegfried Sassoon, Ernest Hemingway, and Ford Maddox Ford, became the canonized writers on the war. As noncombatants, women went into munitions factories and battlefield hospital units, both experiencing and writing dream fantasies of traversing blood-sodden battlefields and losing their own limbs" (Scott, *Gender of Modernism* 6).

Additionally, Scott pinpoints female writers such as Virginia Woolf, Rose Macaulay (author of the 1916 novel *Non-Combatants and Others*), Rebecca West (author of the 1918 novel *Return of the Soldier*), and other female authors who participated in the discourse of war and have recently received more attention as the modernist canon has grown with postmodernism's revisionist work and its inclusion of additional noncombatant war literature. This issue of what actually constitutes combatant or noncombatant war literature is riddled with ambiguity. Matthew Bruccoli points out in *Ernest Hemingway and the Expatriate Movement* that even many of the canonized "war writers," traditionally considered battle participants, who "witnessed the war firsthand did so not as soldiers but as volunteers for first aid agencies," which accounted for what has been described as their often "passive, observational attitude" (18). In discussing the tone and use of irony in modernist literature, Bruccoli notes that the dramatis personae "seem more like spectators than participants in the action" (18). Even though many of the male modernist writers who were veterans expressed a passive attitude toward war, most readers and critics still often favored what they considered "combatant literature," which often meant that it had been written by firsthand observers or veterans of the wars and in many cases offered a detached, negative and, at times, existential view of modern life.

The debate surrounding Willa Cather is one such example of this fight over authenticity. Cather's Pulitzer Prize–winning novel *One of Ours* features the experiences of Claude Hopper, a Midwest boy who finds his calling on the blood-smeared battlefields of France in World War I. Upon its 1922 publication this novel elicited criticism verging, at times, on outrage by male writers such as Ernest Hemingway. In response to *One of Ours*, Hemingway claimed that Cather had not only incorrectly and inaccurately depicted war "using bad Hollywood" (qtd. in Middleton: 84) but had also lifted the war scenes that had any accuracy at all from other texts. Commenting on the novel to Edmund Wilson on November 23, 1923, Hemingway writes, "Look at *One of Ours*. [. . .] Prize, big sale, people taking it seriously. You were in the last war weren't you? Wasn't that last scene in the lines wonderful? Do you know where it came from? The battle scene in *Birth of a Nation*. I identified episode after episode. Catherized. Poor woman, she has to get her war experience somewhere" (qtd. in Middleton: 149). Hemingway's response here captures many of the prevailing prejudices of the era and how some members of the reading public would have responded to a war novel written by a noncombatant woman.

To authors like Hemingway who considered themselves war veterans, Cather's secondhand descriptions of the battlefront experience clearly overstepped the bounds of acceptable subject matter. Perhaps Walker sidestepped some of this criticism because her renditions of the war are safely and consistently filtered through various noncombatant narrators. This narrative choice enabled her to avoid the criticism Cather received, while still allowing her to participate publicly and successfully in the discourse of war.

Stella Deen, in "Rereading the Space Between," an analysis of the temporal and psychological space between the two world wars, discusses modernist writers' destabilization of the "distinctions between male and female spheres so essential to War Office propaganda, [. . .] of public-private distinctions." She concludes that "the war [could] not be limited to the experience of men fighting a series of discrete battles, just as the home front cannot be readily distinguished from the war zone" (8–9). It would appear from these comments that interpretations of modernist war literature, similar to readings of other subjects in modernist literature, have been broadened by postmodernist thought. However, it could also be argued that this broadening was fully underway long before the emergence of postmodernism and was initiated by the modernists themselves.

Walker's novels, for example, often feature characters from both the battle and home fronts and from her own era, and these works received both popular and critical acclaim, none more so than *Winter Wheat*. Interestingly, although this novel is presented in the first-person narrative of a young girl who has not seen the battlefront as the novel starts and has never even left her wind-blown corner of Montana, it is clearly a war novel. By presenting this narrative choice in her novel, Walker subtly demonstrates the wider reaches of war and concomitantly stretches the definition of war literature to include the female sensibility and the domestic milieu. On a similar note, in "Over the Frontier and into the Darkness with Stevie Smith: War, Gender and Identity," an essay in *Challenging Modernism: New Readings in Literature and Culture, 1914–45*, Diana Austin demonstrates how British female writer Stevie Smith (author of *Novel on Yellow Paper* [1936] and *Over the Frontier* [1938]) challenges the concept of war "as a gendering activity" achieved by "reconfiguring the physical war space by shifting the focus to the home front from the battlefront" (36).

Evidently, if there were any trepidation on the part of women authors in the 1940s to participate in the discourse of war, Walker was either outwardly resistant to or perhaps subtly subverting this reluctance. The very fact that she includes an epigraph from Antoine Saint-Exupery's *Flight to Arras* at the start of her novel and divides *Winter Wheat* into three sections, each beginning with quotes from *Flight to Arras*, indicates that she was both aware of and proactive in her participation in the discourse and issues of the day and in other authors' interpretations and dialogue with these issues. Furthermore, the general reading public of her era, in contrast to the New Critics, who would eventually formulate the original modernist canon in which war literature was largely characterized as male and combatant-oriented, were openly receptive to Walker's participation in this discourse. Evidence for this can be found in the healthy sales figure for *Winter Wheat* during the war years. In this novel, the author's presentation of death and other contentious issues typically surrounding war are often offered so factually that readers might easily mistake these depictions as versions of what Hemingway himself criticized as an "observational detachment": the modernist writers' form of shell shock (qtd. in Bruccoli: 19). For example, there are several scenes in *Winter Wheat* when Ellen Webb's reactions to the deaths and pain of those closest to her are sometimes remote or, at the least, understated. For example, after Robert Donaldson, a mentally handicapped student in Ellen's school, wanders off and dies in a snowstorm, Ellen finds herself alone in the teacherage, reliving the event and staring out at the snow. She shares the following:

> It gave me a queer feeling to realize how long I had sat here with my hands idle in my lap [. . .]. What was happening to me? Mom had a funny saying in Russian that she used to mutter under her breath about anyone she thought wasted time brooding over his trouble. She said it was from the Bible and the priests in her village taught it to her. The English of it is:
>
> "A fool folds his hands together and eats away at his own flesh."
>
> I broke away from the trancelike feeling and snapped on the radio. The tinkle of a piano fell on the stillness of my room like the tinkle of breaking glass. I lay on the bed with my hands under my head. The snow fell to music if I looked long enough. (185–86)

Apparently, this is the beginning and ending of Ellen's mourning. To some readers, this abrupt departure from her pain and her thoughts concerning her sense of responsibility for the accident might appear callous. This deceptively hard-nosed reaction to death appears again in *Unless the Wind Turns* and *The Curlew's Cry*. Although the philosophy found in Anna's Russian saying, a close kin to the British "stiff upper lip" and to Walker's own Yankee pragmatism, might offer a possible explanation for these responses to death, the complexity and emotional depth of these characters' reactions to these events belie their callous surface appearances.

For instance, in *Winter Wheat*, when Anna tells her daughter about her parents' deaths in Russia during the war, her story is factual and succinct and offers some explanation for Ellen's subsequent reactions to Robert's tragic death. In fact, as Ellen considers Robert's death, she recalls a day she and her mother spent in the garden. An eight-year-old Ellen had asked her mother, "Are my grandparents living, Mom?" In the clipped dialogue that follows this question and through a young Ellen's reactions, Walker demonstrates how the horrors of war could touch even a young girl in central Montana and, at the same time, lays the foundation for Ellen's own survival in the face of future tragedies:

> "They was both killed," Mom said [. . .].
>
> "Killed, Mom?" I couldn't believe it. Children in Gotham had their grandparents living with them. How could mine have been killed? [. . .]
>
> "What did you do, Mom?"
>
> "My brother and I live in old shack for while. Then he go to be a priest. I help nurse wounded soldiers." [. . .]
>
> Mom was through talking, but all afternoon in the hot rows [as they weeded the beets] I thought about my grandmother and grandfather, part of me, killed. (33–34)

That afternoon, through her mother's clipped words, Ellen metaphorically sees the same red blood that dripped into the Russian earth in the leaves of beets that they weed. Throughout the novel, the war literally keeps popping up. For instance, pieces of the imbedded shrapnel Ben Webb carries deeply within his flesh from World War I wounds emerge, causing him and the rest of the family great discomfort. Again, metaphorically, this image of the shrapnel illustrates the unending pain and deep-buried wounds of war that affect all family members.

Despite this reoccurring ugliness, however, Walker is also able to demonstrate that our inhumanity to one another and its subsequent effects do not extinguish human hope or the sense of decency human beings have for one another. Readers also learn from the conversation between Ellen and her mother that day in the beet patch that Anna Petrovna's brother did not turn away from his God despite the fact that his family and many others had been shot and burnt to death and that Anna, although hardened by these events, did not become shell shocked or indifferent to humanity, but instead found consolation from her losses by nursing the wounded soldiers and by creating a new life in Montana. Readers also learn that although modern warfare may have cauterized Anna's free-flowing expression, it did not extinguish her humane beliefs or her deepest emotions.

Winter Wheat offers both noncombatants' and combatants' views on war, filtered through the voice of a young Ellen Webb. This character, because of her innocence and wholly secondhand retellings of others' experiences, is able to inhabit, through her narrative, the worlds of both those who once served on the front and those who experience the war in the far reaches of the American heartland. Additionally, this first-person narrator in *Winter Wheat* enabled Walker to avoid the criticism directed at *One of Ours*, with its limited omniscient voice that tacitly demanded an assumption on the part of readers of a greater level of personal knowledge. Because of this narrative choice in *Winter Wheat*, its readers, both male and female, combatants and noncombatants, remained receptive to and unthreatened by both the narrative voice of Ellen Webb and the female consciousness and authority of Walker behind that voice. Readers find this balance again in a scene in the novel that openly explores a soldier's mind and his thoughts on war when Ellen asks her father about the conflict as he recovers from another painful episode with his shrapnel wounds:

> I was glad Dad felt enough better to talk, but I wasn't much interested at first. Then I remembered how he had said to Mom that night: "If there hadn't been a war, we wouldn't be here. I wouldn't be a physical wreck." My mind felt stealthy and sharp.
>
> "I wouldn't think you could forgive the last war for . . . for this Dad?"
>
> "Why not? You have to take a chance. Other men had lots worse things than this." Dad's voice was mild and unresentful.
>
> "Do you wish you had never been a soldier, Dad? You would be back in Vermont, wouldn't you?"
>
> Dad lit a cigarette. "Yes, I presume I'd be still in the East; probably teaching somewheres. There are things I wouldn't have missed though."
>
> I felt a little ashamed, but I asked anyway. "What things, Dad?"
>
> "Oh, a lot of things, Ellen. It was a pretty big thrill sailing for Europe when I was nineteen, feeling the world was counting on me, I felt sorry for the boys back in Plainville whose parents wouldn't let them go. You had to have your parents consent if you were that young.
>
> "Oh, it wasn't all patriotism, I don't suppose. My family was very strict. When I was home I couldn't miss church or stay out with a girl after seven o'clock or drink or smoke, I liked being free and on my own. Some people didn't think of the Army as letting you be very free, but I did."
>
> "And I had a good time with the other men in my company, fellows I would have never known in Plainville. There was a fellow named Josef Podoroski, a Polack from Hamtramck, Michigan. He'd worked since he was fourteen in a factory. I wouldn't ever have met him if it hadn't been for the Army. I never liked a man so well."
>
> "Where is he now Dad?"
>
> "He was killed in that fracas Armistice Day when I got this bird shot in me." (108)

This passage demonstrates both Ellen's negative feelings about war—she is a bit ashamed to think that her father says "There are things I wouldn't have missed though"—and, at the same time, also exposes Ben Webb's more positive viewpoints on his involvement as he candidly discusses his freedom and friendships that resulted from his time as a soldier. For example, despite Josef Podoroski's death, Ben Webb continues to value his war experiences and views the liberalization that came with the army as positive aspects of the experience; to be able to smoke, drink, stay out with a girl, and miss church are all aspects of modern life that emerged from his direct participation in the war.

Later in the text, with the outbreak of World War II, Walker will once again use Ellen's narrative voice to present divergent viewpoints of war. With the bombing of Pearl Harbor, Ellen watches in shock as her father and mother sit glued to the radio. She comments, "Dad was so excited I felt ashamed that I was so quiet. I had never heard war declared before; I had only read about it. Mom sat down on the couch, listening to every word. Her eyes flashed, but she didn't say anything" (204). In reviewing the cryptic remarks from each family that follow in this scene, it is helpful to remember the compression and complexity of action and meaning in modernist texts. Regarding the male-female dichotomy of war and the gendering of war literature, Austin, in an essay on author Stevie Smith, notes:

> Males are automatically at the center of war discourse, because, whether soldiers or non-combatants, they have to position themselves actively in relation to what is seen by many as the quintessential test of their culture's values and of their own manhood. Women, however, are automatically relegated to the margins. As the political philosopher Bethke Elshtain observes, man is assigned to the active role of "Just Warrior," and adapting a Hegelian term, woman is construed as the passive keeper of the flame of non-warlike values. (36)

In keeping with Austin's observations, it is notable that in the Webb household, Ben moves in closer to the radio with Warren (the neighbor), while Ellen picks up a book of poetry and retreats to the other room. The men are the "warriors," while she is "the passive keeper of the flame of non-warlike values." However, Anna stands somewhere between the two. She witnessed war atrocities, as did her husband, and suffered even more directly than he. Readers might question Anna's physical and emotional position in this middle ground, "*as though* she were interested in every word" (205; italics added). Some readers might interpret Anna's positioning near the radio and the men as proof that Ellen's mother is akin to the patriarchal, patriotic mothers who send their sons off to their deaths, as fictionalized in *Mrs. Dalloway*. But perhaps there is another reason Anna stands there "as though she were interested." She might not be remembering the horrible details of the war as she jokes with her husband but instead their first kiss with the announcement of the previous armistice. From Anna's and Ben's reactions to the news of Pearl Harbor, readers learn that the horrors of the First World War are already a distant and somewhat romanticized memory for these two characters. Somehow, the past has a romanticism that even a harsh realist like Anna is unable to entirely escape. Ellen, however, being much younger, is not caught in this romantic glow. "They were fools," she remarks before storming off to her room. This scene also captures the intergenerational conflict arising from different perceptions of the same events.

Along with chronicling various reactions to the news of Pearl Harbor, Walker uses this same passage to expose other contentious issues surrounding war and its rhetoric. She employs irony in Ben's comment about war being good for commodity prices and in Anna's retort that, in the end, wars are expensive and bad for economies, perhaps to remind her readers of the complexity of all wars and of the confusion between patriotism, idealism, and economics. In fact, Walker does not forget to remind her readers that Ellen is only able to return to college because of the escalating grain prices brought on by the war. Even this innocent young girl, who wants only to be educated and peacefully productive, seems to receive her education as a result of the war.

Perhaps not coincidentally, just before the family hears the news of Pearl Harbor, Ben Webb has been outside, getting the numbers off his combine so that he can mortgage it to raise much-needed tuition money. However, being out in the cold Montana air causes his wounds to flare up again. The novelist's positioning of this scene immediately before the announcement of Pearl Harbor compresses the time between these two wars. Readers might wonder, as Ellen must, if there were two wars or one Great War with a short intermission. And, although Warren is a young man and Ben is middle-aged, their age differences fade as they sit by the radio.

Tellingly, as he sits there, Ellen's father does not hear Ellen's question, which must have been on everyone's minds when war again erupted shortly after the anniversary of the armistice of "the war to end all wars." Ben might not have answered Ellen's questions because he did not hear them. If this were the case, Walker may be commenting on how the news, rhetoric, and excitement of the war literally drowned out the harsh realities of the previous one and all its implications. Or, in having Ben not answer his daughter, the author may also be demonstrating that the previous generation has no answers to the next generation's questions. By having Ellen ask whether all the efforts and loss of the previous war had been in vain and, if so, what the point in fighting again was, the author poses universal questions for her characters and readers—questions that are perhaps universally unanswerable.

In positioning a younger healthy man, Warren, alongside war-injured Ben, Walker demonstrates another irony of war. At first, Warren seems to believe he will remain impervious to injuries or death. Although Warren remains unscathed as the novel closes, the other young man in the novel—Gil, Ellen's first beau—has already enlisted and died. Initially, Warren is caught up in the romanticism of war, much as Gil had been.

This upsets Ellen, just as any sentimentality bothered Walker herself. These same issues of blind patriotism and romanticism are again addressed later in the text when Warren comes into Ellen's school after a drinking binge the night before he must return to his military position. First he reminisces to Ellen about how he received his early education in the very same one-room schoolhouse where they sit:

> "I can tell you the dates of all the wars America ever fought and why we fought 'em and why we're going to fight this one. Isn't this school the cradle of America? Sure! And how the politician loves it!" He swung his arm in a wide gesture and his voice was loud.
>
> "Citizens of the United States, look to the little red schoolhouse if you would safeguard the future of America. Teach 'em the Gettysburg Address and Washington's Farewell Address an' you won't lack for soldiers to fight your battles. If they don't do well as private citizens, that won't matter now. They'll win the war. America always wins her wars.
>
> "But we've got to learn more than that in the little red schoolhouse; got to learn how to live decently afterward, too." [. . .]
>
> "When you're a kid in school here, you want to be great and famous," he went on, but his voice lost its ranting note. "After a while you go away and you forget about that. You want someone to love you the way you love her and you want to make a good living, and live a decent life. When you don't get that, then you're ready to settle for some ideas, but they have to be good ones. That's when a man goes in for religion, I guess, some kind of a faith. But you can't pick up faith at a cut-rate drugstore. A man's lucky if there's a war on that he can go and fight in. If he gets killed in it, his life'll do some good, maybe." (245–46)

In his drunken and candid ranting, Warren not only exposes the complexity of what on the surface appears to be a "blind patriotism" on the part of many enlistees but also demonstrates the need that soldiers have for love, a good life, faith, and strength, so that they may continue to truly believe they are fighting for these things. In this passage, readers glimpse the more existential version of modernist viewpoints, with Warren's discrediting of his education, which he claims he now views largely as propaganda, and of religion and love, which he now claims are now impossibly out of reach. Death on the battleground, Warren adds, appears to be the only meaningful outcome for his life. After this dramatic claim, Ellen dismisses his outburst, knowing full well that he doesn't mean all that he is saying; if he did, she reasons, he wouldn't have had any reason to make the long drive to her school to declare all these thoughts to her.

With emotional scenes such as these, some readers might wonder where the author herself stood in the midst of all these different perspectives on war. An answer to this might possibly be found in a conversation she once had with her daughter. As they were discussing a character in one of her novels, Walker surprised her daughter by claiming, "Why, all my characters are noble!" "Noble" was an interesting word to choose. An explanation for her use of "noble" might be found in the thoughts of another author who used this same word. In a discussion on technique and Sarah Orne Jewett, Willa Cather wrote, "If he [the author] achieves anything *noble*, anything enduring, it must be by giving himself absolutely to his material. And this gift of sympathy is his great gift; it is the fine thing in him that alone can make his work fine" (qtd. in Middleton: 34; italics added). This sympathetic ability to maintain the complexity and integrity of each character is a trademark of Walker's fiction. Although she studies both the positive and negative characteristics of the individuals in her novels, she consistently refuses to either vilify or sentimentalize any of them. They remain human, with both laudable and damning qualities, and are both realistically human and "noble," endowed with all the ambiguities and conundrums their own creator confronted.

For example, although it would be tempting to read some of the above excerpts of *Winter Wheat* as criticisms of the male gendering of war, Warren's final outburst undercuts that earlier temptation. In her introduction to *The Gender of Modernism*, Bonnie Kime Scott reminds her readers of Virginia Woolf's Lily Briscoe, "who seeks in feminine territory some secret which people must have for the world to go on at all," an "aim," she claims, "shared by many modernists" (16). Walker might have sought this "secret" but would not have thought of it as wholly "feminine." By revealing the complex thoughts of Warren Harper and by showing how men also nurture hope, she demonstrates that the "secret" is by no means exclusively gendered as "feminine territory."

The scene in *Winter Wheat* depicting the announcement of Pearl Harbor and Ellen's retreat into her room with a book of poetry is noteworthy in a discussion of "the feminine" in modernist war fiction. Despite witnessing Ellen retreat as she did from the room, readers in no way sense that she flees from her own engagement with the war. In her room, her thoughts and Walt Whitman's poetry encompass much of what she has seen and heard. Her choice of Whitman's poetry and his discourses on the Civil War indicates that her departure was not a retreat, but rather, her own form of engagement.

There is one repetition in *Winter Wheat* that illustrates Walker's feelings on war. Throughout the novel, Ellen uses the word "ashamed." She declares that she is ashamed of her father's romanticism and many of his comments on the war. She reiterates that she is ashamed of her mother's comments and also of her neighbors' fervor over the war. Shame is what repeats itself. This was what the next generation, Walker among them, felt: shame for what they were, for their histories, and for where they were headed.

6. The Mothers of Modernism

In his critical introduction to *The Brewers' Big Horses*, David Budbill refers to its protagonist, Sara Henkel, as "a nascent feminist" because of her independent spirit and the confidence she shows in taking on roles typically set aside for men in the early days of the twentieth century (viii). These include riding a bike, insisting upon taking a job at the local newspaper, marrying outside her family's social circle, and eventually running a brewery. Similarly, in her critical introduction to *Light from Arcturus*, Mary Swander approaches the character Julia Hauser by noting that "from a current feminist viewpoint, *Light from Arcturus* not only gives us a historical perspective on 'trailing spouses' but on women's selfhood" (x). Mary Clearman Blew, in her 1987 essay on *The Curlew's Cry*, offers another observation about Walker's feminist characters that stresses the recurring theme she discovered in the novel concerning the dominance wielded by western men over western women (qtd in Hugo: 186). Despite the fact that Mildred Walker was either uncomfortable or in disagreement with these feminist interpretations of her novels, there can be no doubt that she, like her character Sara Henkel, can be considered at first glance and at the very least a nascent feminist in both how she lived and in the characters she created. However, a closer inspection here indicates that Walker's form of feminism may have been more than nascent, and instead might be interpreted as a sophisticated and complex gender-volatile viewpoint that rejected the traditional binary of male versus female or the feminine versus the masculine and instead favored a complex questioning of gender and the potentially androgynous nature of human beings. With her frequent infusion of the question of gender in her texts, Walker contributes to the feminist discourse of twentieth-century literature that Bonnie Kime Scott and the contributors to *The Gender of Modernism* consider integral to modernism's growth and definition. In her introduction to *The Gender of Modernism*, Scott suggests that the use of the word "gender" is more helpful than the traditional critical use of the binaries "feminine" and "masculine" because "[g]ender is a category constructed through cultural and social systems. Unlike sex, it is not a biological fact determined at conception. [. . .] Gender is more fluid, flexible, and multiple in its options than the (so far) unchanging biologically binary of male and female" (2). In her essay "Toward a Gendered Reading of Modernism," Scott remarks: "Modernism as caught in the mesh of gender is polyphonic, mobile, interactive, sexually charged; it has wide appeal, constituting a historic shift in parameters" (4). The parameters Scott refers to defined the previously limited versions of modernism: the "early male modernism," with its experimental, audience challenging, and language-focused writing, or modernism as an "outsider's society," with its own clear group identifications.

Scott's claims can be better understood in light of the complexity of Walker's stance. Although in life Walker seemed to reject feminist readings of her novels, her fiction by no means resists these interpretations, offering numerous presentations of independent-minded women with individual agency over many aspects of their less-than-traditional lives. Walker's own rejection of these feminist interpretations might be due (at least in part) to the reaction she and other authors may have felt toward much of the feminist criticism in the mid–twentieth century. To be sure, throughout the many years of her career, the term "feminism" was by no means static, nor is it today.

As a young woman, Walker clearly reaped many of the benefits of the efforts to establish the rights of the "New Women." The women who struggled for women's rights prior to the turn of the century were successful in attaining many of their goals by the time Walker completed grade school. By this time, higher education had become a reality for more women than in the past, as did participation in the middle-class work force. Feminist scholar Marylu Hill notes that these "new possibilities for education and work were joined in the 1890s by a growing feminist challenge to societal attitudes—the advent of the New Woman" (6). These included the rights of unmarried girls to be considered "individuals as well as daughters"—to make their own errors, to travel, and to dare to attempt to seize male power through such symbolic actions as smoking, bicycling, and altering their dress and demeanor. However, by 1910, these New Women already seemed the outdated older sisters of the next generation. In both life and fiction they were often stereotyped in their struggles for independence as angry, frustrated, defeated, or dead. Marylu Hill suggests that the modern woman, distinguished from the New Woman, believed that "life and fiction offered new more interesting and often positive alternatives" other than defeat, death, anger, or frustration (*Mothering Modernity* 1). Additionally, in *New Women, New Novels*, Ann Ardis argues that the New Women were by no means a homogenous group and that such generalizations misrepresent the complexity of the movement. Furthermore, Ardis explains that the experimentation and heterogeneous nature of the New Women in society and in fiction had much to do with the rise of modernism itself. However, having said all this, Ardis still distinguishes these earlier "New Women" as a particular type of group from those women that follow. She writes: "It is worth emphasizing that the twentieth century writers did not always invoke the same legacy as they produced new riffs on the theme of the New Women [. . .]. [T]he twentieth century ushered in a new generation of writers who now became involved in this old controversy over the New Women," [who were, in fact, by this time the old New Women] (169).

Walker began her adult life in this subsequent generation of heterogeneous New Women. The fact that she was able to attend, on a scholarship, Wells College, a private and enlightened women's college in upstate New York, was an indication of the benefits she received in her own career from the struggles of these earlier feminists. Once she was within this educational and protected system that encouraged young women to consider and create their own futures, Walker once again received the nurturing of independence and confidence that her predecessors had fought for so vociferously. The fact that, when she left university, she began her own career in advertising copywriting and only agreed to marry under the condition that she could continue her own career as a writer is evidence of her own sense of confidence, destiny, and independence, no doubt nurtured during her earlier years at Wells College. In light of her debt to the early feminist movement, readers must question why the author responded so negatively to feminist interpretations of her novels.

Her response needs to be placed within the context of its time. Mary Clearman Blew wrote her essay on *The Curlew's Cry* in 1987. Mary Swander wrote her introduction to *Light from Arcturus* in the early 1990s. By this era, feminism had come to take on many different meanings than it had in the previous decades. The 1960s and 1970s were noteworthy for their public protests, of which some feminists were part. The "either/or" and "anti-" rhetoric dominated the dialogue in this era, and the most highly visible contingency of the feminist movement was characterized by charismatic and high-profile spokespeople such as Gloria Steinem, marches and demonstrations in the streets, public bra-burnings, and the use of terms such as "male chauvinist pig." These more public aspects of feminist reform had many similarities to the suffragettes' movement at the turn of the century, with both causes advocating similar participation in many other social reforms of the day. By the late 1980s, Walker would most likely have associated the term "feminist" with these public protests and the high profile events of the previous two decades, with which she would not have felt partisan. It might be said that Walker was born too late to be a "suffragette" and too early to be a "women's libber." Caught in this middle ground, she appears to have rejected the posturing of both social movements despite that fact that her work, similar to Cather's, benefited from the struggles of both groups and eras. Despite her comments and her outward rejection of feminist readings of her novels, she clearly did not reject the growing independence of women and society's evolving viewpoints on gender—neither in her own life nor in the lives of her novels' characters.

By inspecting more closely the novelist's responses to the comments of Mary Swander and Mary Clearman Blew, it becomes apparent that Walker objected primarily to the sense of the polarity these critics suggested—of women against men, or the male versus the female sensibility. To disavow the binary, however, does not mean that she did not believe in pursuing her own understanding of gender studies, one that was more complex than this "either / or" binary approach.

For instance, in the scene in *Winter Wheat* when Ellen Webb takes the wheel from her boyfriend, who is incapable of steering the farm truck out of a muddy section of road, some readers might see this as the female appropriating what is typically a man's role: driving a big truck. However, as the novel progresses, Ellen realizes that her differences with Gil do not stem from their separate genders but, instead, to differences in their upbringings, and she begins to understand that he has never driven a farm truck before because of his urban upbringing and that it is her familiarity with the vehicle, rather than anything about gender, that enables her to succeed in an action that is traditionally—and incorrectly—considered male. Likewise, Sara Henkel in *The Brewers' Big Horses* is depicted as crossing traditionally gendered activities when she takes over the operations of the family brewery. When Sara's husband dies and she is forced to take the helm of the family brewery, her family assumes she will do so in name only. But when Sara surprises everyone with her hands-on approach to business, she is, ironically, most ridiculed by her female suffragette acquaintances and family members. To her family, feminism implies that the female must appropriate the male roles and join forces with the patriarchal society and become what Marylu Hill refers to as a "little man," a "creature less than female, yet still not male" (5). If, in fact, Walker's novels ended solely with these female characters' business successes, a reader might easily conclude that the novelist demonstrated this form of feminist understanding and that her characters' successes as "little men" maintained the binary of feminine / masculine. However, these novels do not end with the successes of "little men." Despite their business accomplishments, the women in Walker's novels remain unfulfilled and still seek additional fulfillment of what is traditionally considered their more "feminine sides." These female characters also seek love, understanding, and nurturing. In Sara Henkel's case, her story ends with the possibility of her bending her hardened and independent-minded resolve and finally accepting the help and friendship of a male. It is clear in this novel that until both the demands of the outer world (business commitments) and those of the inner world (the need for a deep sharing with other human beings) are satisfied, there can be no resolution. In fact, this is the case with all of Walker's protagonists, male or female. It is in this compromise that readers find the modernist novelist's complex explorations of gender and advanced theories of feminism.

As Scott indicates, the conception of gender changes in history, across cultures, and in the lifetime of an individual, as it did for Walker (2). From her first novel through her last, Walker explored the question of gender from different angles: from the perspectives of young, married, and single women, elderly and disabled individuals, children, and men. For instance, *Fireweed*, *Light from Arcturus*, *The Brewers' Big Horses*, and *The Orange Tree* focus on recently married young women and their own developing perspectives on gender for both themselves and those around them as they embark on their lives as wives, mothers, and members of a community. *Dr. Norton's Wife*, *Medical Meeting*, *Unless the Wind Turns*, *The Body of a Young Man*, *If a Lion Could Talk*, and *The Orange Tree* capture the complex feelings of middle-aged couples as circumstances force them to reevaluate their own roles and those of the people around them. *The Southwest Corner* captures an elderly women's reevaluation of gender as she approaches her final days. *Winter Wheat*, *The Curlew's Cry*, *A Piece of the World*, and *The Quarry* begin with a presentation of their protagonists (both male and female) as children. As these adolescents mature, readers are privy to these characters' confusions, reevaluations of gender, and their ever-changing roles as members of different groups and communities.

One of the more interesting struggles coming out of the author's own exploration of gender can be found in these younger female characters' evolving relationships with their mothers. An examination of these mother-daughter relationships reveals many of the author's own varying explorations and evolving viewpoints on the issue of gender. Repeatedly in these novels, the mother figures are rejected by their daughters, Walker's young, female protagonists. In this sense, these young women appear "orphan-like," as do many modernist characters. But, on closer examination, a reader discovers that each of these women experiences first the inevitable break with the mother and the past and then, always, the journey back to her biological mother or to a mother figure.

In *Mothering Modernity* Marylu Hill discusses similar journeys created by other modernist writers. Beginning with Dorothy Richardson's *Pointed Rooves* and moving on to E. M. Forster's *Howard's End* and Virginia Woolf's *To the Lighthouse*, Hill argues that although the female characters in these novels seem to move into a traditionally male space, their growth is not satisfied until they make some return to the mother figures they initially rejected. She adds that their journeys into the male realm are to "appropriate the father tongue [. . .] so to speak [. . .] to recover the heretofore silenced mother" (4). In her study of Richardson's *Pilgrimage*, Hill suggests that Miriam's journey "seeks integration of disparate inheritances from both father and mother" (4). In this novel, Miriam alters her opinions by initially experiencing frustration with other females and harboring a subsequent wish to be like a man, to then imagining herself almost sexless and plain, to then experiencing a revelation resulting from an encounter with a friend's illness. Miriam finds that she can no longer dismiss the hysteria she witnessed in earlier years from her own mother and other women but instead must try to understand sympathetically how these women had been weighed down with thoughts and suppressions that brought them to the brink their apparent madness. Later in the novel, Miriam finds herself longing to return to some sense of her mother. Eventually, Miriam realizes that even though many women conform superficially to the world around them, they still manage to maintain a submerged sense of womanhood and of independent thoughts and dreams, and that this submergence and suppression are often the causes of their hysteria and madness (82).

A number of Walker's female protagonists also take journeys similar to Miriam's in *Pilgrimage*. Walker's characters not only find a voice for silenced mothers but also develop a voice for the new persona of their own emerging self-creation, a blend of both the male and the female in the traditional binary with a unique, modern permutation that eliminates the "either / or." Similarly, later in her discussion in "From New Women to Modernists," scholar Marylu Hill concludes: "I do intend to take this [discussion of recovery] one step further and suggest that not only do the young women in these novels rediscover the mother, but they also seek to bring the mother into modernity as a method of redefining themselves and their world" [—in an act of self-creation] (14).

Hill explains further how "[c]ertain key characteristics of the mother—characteristics fostered by centuries of domesticity and women's relationships—are revealed as the crucial antithesis to contemporary history. These characteristics include a cyclical, non-linear awareness of time and history; a tendency to silence; an attention to the personal rather than the impersonal; and an awareness that privileges both / and configurations rather than and / or" (14). On a similar note, in "Women's Time," the feminist critic Julia Kristeva argues that women's time is unique in that it is characterized by cycles, gestations, and recurrences of biological rhythms in tune with nature, rather than linear time. Furthermore, Kristeva argues that because of women's experiences of motherhood—of gestation and nurturing their young—there is therefore no clear line separating the world inside and the one outside, encouraging a vision of a world more in line with "both / and" rather than "either / or." Walker employed these flashbacks and other literary devices to defy the linearity of time and delineation of subject in her novels, especially in her later ones.

In *Spaces of the Mind*, Elaine Jahner approaches some of these same issues concerning self-creation and the roles of mothers in her discussion of *Winter Wheat* through formalist discourse theory. Jahner arrives at many of the same conclusions as the feminist critics mentioned previously, one of which being that Ellen, after she leaves home (and her mother), must reevaluate language and understanding to form her own language separate from that of her mother, and that she must actively seek a form of self-creation. On this subject, Jahner writes: "Walker gives us maternal characters who prompt questions about what a person's place in a family might have to do with that person's ability to find a place within a landscape and within the narrative whose significance has to be found in that landscape. Is there [. . .] always and necessarily a secret dimension to a mother's love that binds a child to a place even as it frees that child from infantile dependence on the mother?" (141).

In her own life, Walker, similar to many of her female protagonists, seemed to reject the mother figure and often favored the opinions and the company of men over women. She herself admitted to her daughter that her own father—and not her mother—was by far the greatest influence in her life. This proclivity of her mother continues to trouble Ripley Hugo, and she dedicates various sections of her biography to this specific issue. At one point Hugo reminisces:

> As Mother told her stories, I often sensed an attitude that accorded her mother the accomplishment of keeping a house but not much more, not anything particularly admirable or instructive. When I was older, she told me that her mother could always reduce the amount of ingredients called for in a recipe [. . .]. It annoyed her that "shorting" recipe ingredients [. . .] should be a matter of pride. What Mother scorned was her mother's desire to retire to Vermont and raise chickens. "Chickens!" Mother would say when she mentioned this. "How awful that would be." I did wonder about Mother's distaste because, after all, we later raised chickens when we lived in Montana. [. . .] Now I imagine that Mother preferred not to think of herself as having a mother with such uninteresting ambitions as making do or raising chickens. [. . .]
>
> Mother's stories about her father, in contrast, were always told with pride. Each vignette of him from her childhood emphasized how carefully, even exactingly, he coached her important skills. [. . .] She told us when we were grown, almost inadvertently and with shy pride, that her father called her 'Peter'. He had wanted her to be a boy, she said matter-of-factly. He explained to her that Peter was his favorite name because Peter was one of the finest apostles as well as a fisherman. I sensed that being 'Peter' assured her that she had a special role to fulfill for her father, perhaps of succeeding in a way that a girl would not be expected to, a way that set her apart from her sister. (Hugo 6–9)

From Hugo's thoughts, her mother's alliance with the male world is both apparent and perhaps understandable. However, if the comments Walker made about her own life are held up alongside her fiction, a world more complex than this binary division emerges. Regarding the comment about raising chickens, Hugo acknowledges that they did, in fact, raise poultry on their acreage in Montana. Although the dirty work was not Walker's job, she did encourage her children in this and similar endeavors. Given her vehemence on the subject and rejection of her mother's values, it is interesting that she encouraged her children to take part in this less "ambitious" activity. It may have been that Walker's rhetoric with her daughter about her own mother's interests and way of life were not actually indicative of the author's own, more genuine feelings.

Paralleling the complexities in Walker's own life, the daughter in *Winter Wheat* finally comes to understand and accept her mother and feel an adult closeness to her when they share in butchering and dressing turkeys for Christmas. Coincidentally, this activity has many similarities to the author's memories of her mother raising chickens. In recreating this scene, Walker may have attempted to create a resolution with her own mother and issues concerning that female figure. She may have sought a sense of wholeness that she knew she could never achieve solely through success in "the male world," understanding intuitively the inherent limitations of being the "little man," and recognizing the necessity for "self-creation" that could only come with some resolution and reevaluation of the mother figure.

In *Winter Wheat* Ellen Webb narrates her experiences during a two-year period. This includes the season prior to leaving home, her year away at college, and her subsequent winter of solitude at a teacherage and school, plus her eventual return to the family home. During this time, Ellen meets her beau's family and is exposed to women who are more genteel and traditional than her mother and to homes filled with music, art, and other aspects of refined culture—in stark contrast to her own childhood home. Upon returning home, Ellen sees her life through the lens of this other world and is disappointed by the coarseness of her mother and her home. As Ellen's first love affair falters, she looks critically at the relationship between her parents for possible explanations and blame. Under the misguided impression that her mother's appearance and demeanor are largely responsible for her fiancé's rejection, Ellen delves deeply and critically into her mother's life. She even goes so far in her thoughts as to convince herself that her mother lied to her father about a false pregnancy and thereby forced him into an unhappy marriage. In her critical adolescent moments Ellen can imagine no other reason why her father would have married Anna. The fact that Anna is not talkative exasperates Ellen and amplifies her misconceptions. With these tortured thoughts, Ellen even begins to resent the time she must spend in the house cooking, cleaning, and caring for her father, roles she perceives incorrectly as belonging solely to her mother. Despite Ellen's thoughts, however, Anna's world extends far beyond this stereotypically domestic female space. In fact, what Ellen does not understand at the time is that what she actually—and ironically—rejects is her mother's lack of weakness and "femininity" and her ability to turn her hand independently to almost any task. Stronger than her war-injured father, Ellen's mother can stack hay for hours and then come in and cook a meal and tend to her ailing husband without complaint. Ellen blames her failed engagement on the fact that her mother does not represent the traditionally weak female and consequently has not provided her with an appropriate role model to succeed in a more urban environment. It is only when the two women are left alone for Christmas that the underlying reason for Ellen's rejection of her mother becomes more apparent to both Ellen and the novel's readers.

Throughout the novel, Ellen awakens to her own female physical longings. During her year at university she has her first serious relationship with a man, and she later comes to know a number of other men. As Ellen wrestles with her own maturity and sense of femininity and navigates through the difficult terrain of her adolescence, she inherently fears becoming her mother. She thinks Gil rejected her because she was too coarse, too practical, and too much like her mother and not at all like Gil's mother or the other women Ellen met at college, who appeared more feminine.

When Walker describes the business of butchering the turkeys, noting the scalding water, the pin feathers, the guts, and the mess, there is nothing but hard, coarse work in this chore, epitomizing both how Ellen sees her mother's life and how she fears her own life will go. At this point in the novel, Ellen is at her lowest ebb, without prospects for a future education because of family finances and without the hope of an escape to a softer life through marriage. Readers learn that Ellen's mother raises the turkeys each year as a means to earn money for Christmas gifts. As the women finish dressing the turkeys, Ellen notices that her mother carefully ties strings of uncooked red cranberries around each neck. Ellen also remembers that her father had laughed at the strings of cranberries last year but had understood that the customers always appreciated them. Although the "cranberries were dear" that year, Anna continues to tie the superfluous berries on the turkeys' necks (224). This act causes Ellen to reconsider her previous thoughts and to appreciate her mother's gratuitous and artistic gestures. Shaken from her previously negative thoughts by this revelation, Ellen begins to observe her mother both from a greater distance and with a more discerning and appreciative perspective. No longer solely the daughter but also a young woman and companion as they drive to town, Ellen fingers the little identification tags her mother has written and tied to each turkey. As an indication of her new vision, Ellen notes, "It dawned on me today as I looked down on the notebook in her hands that Dad must have taught her how to write" and [to speak English] (226). Not coincidentally, at this point in the narrative, a Chinook has blown in from the mountains, warming both the air and Ellen's heart. At this point Ellen begins to appreciate the difficulties her mother must have faced both as a young immigrant assimilating into a foreign culture and as a woman simultaneously seeking her own self-identity.

When the women are finished delivering the turkeys, they go to the store to buy presents for Christmas. They decide to buy each other coats. First, Anna chooses a coat for Ellen. Still critical, Ellen decides bitterly that her mother has given her this coat solely because the price has been slashed. Then, Ellen's thoughts are interrupted when her mother spots a red coat for herself, and she observes:

> I saw the saleswoman thought it [the red coat] was too young for Mom, but she had already put it on. She walked over in front of the glass and for the first time in my life I saw she must have liked clothes, too. [. . .]
>
> "You like it, Yelena?"
>
> "Yes, I believe I do," I said, looking at Mom in a new way. It's hard for a daughter to realize that her mother could still be young. [. . .]
>
> "It's the color of the cranberries we put on the turkeys, Yeléna," she said. [. . .]
>
> "Ben like red," Mom said [. . .]. (228)

In this poignant scene, Ellen moves even closer to both her mother and a fuller understanding of herself. She realizes that even though her mother can plow a field and butcher animals, these activities cannot extinguish her softer and perhaps more frivolous side that hangs red berries on a turkey's neck and sets flowering geraniums on the bare kitchen windowsills just because they are pretty. Aware of her mother's displacement from her native homeland, without the support of others with the same cultural background, and without the comforts of a familiar religion or language, Ellen begins to appreciate that Anna's new life in Montana had been stripped down to the bare essentials. As such, her reinvention of herself and her sense of gender contained only what was essential for her survival. Her identity might be characterized as both male and female but is, in fact, neither. Anna pragmatically balances the requirements for survival in a harsh and lonely landscape alongside the human needs for beauty, love, and acceptance and creates a unique gendering of herself. At this point in the novel, Ellen realizes that she will also forge her own identity, not because it has been forced upon her, but because she now understands herself and can make better choices. Although Ellen's growing awareness of this complex and creative side of her mother does not lead to an immediate reconciliation with her, it points the young woman toward a fuller sense of gender, to reconciliation between her mother and herself, and to an eventual creation of gender and identity.

Ellen and Anna's ultimate reconciliation occurs after Ellen has received a letter indicating that Gil has been killed in action. Ellen keeps this fact to herself and allows her confusion and anger to fester. As Ellen helps her mother whitewash the chicken coop, her emotions finally explode. Implicit in Ellen's hostility toward her mother throughout the narrative has been the young woman's belief that her mother somehow tricked her father into marriage. Furthermore, Ellen believes this proves that there is no real love in the Webb household, that all their lives are built on lies and are as ugly as withered crops, and that outsiders can see all this clearly and are therefore repelled by them—as Gil had been. Ellen's frustrations finally erupt:

> "I'm not like you, Mom, so I'd do anything to get a man to marry me!"
>
> Mom held her brush still. She looked at me so blankly it made me all the angrier. I couldn't stop then.
>
> "Don't look as though you didn't know what I was talking about. I know how you tricked Dad. I overheard you the night after Gil left. I know he married you and took you back to America because you told him you were pregnant. Then you made him bring you out here on this ranch where he never wanted to come. And when he knew you weren't

> going to have a child it was too late. He was married to you, and he was too honorable to go away and leave you."
>
> I couldn't seem to stop. I watched my words fall like blows on Mom's face. I don't think she took in all I said; I talked too fast. Mom couldn't understand if a person didn't speak slowly.
>
> "And you've gone on all these years hating each other. Gil felt that hate. He could tell just being here. That's one of the things that drove him away from here, from me." I almost choked on my own words. I guess I was crying. I sat down on an old box and covered my face.
>
> Mom was still so long I looked up at her. All the color had gone out of her face, except in her eyes. She shook her head.
>
> "You don't know anything, Yeléna. [. . .] In our church if baby is not christened we say she go blind in next world. I think you go blind in this world—blind dumb!" She stopped and then went on slowly. "No, Yeléna, I never hate Ben an' Ben don't hate me. *Gospode Boge*! I love him here so all these years!" Mom touched her breast and her face broke into life. Here eyes were softer. "Me hate Ben!" She laughed. I sat there dumbly watching her. Her laughter seemed far away [. . .].
>
> "But, Mom, I heard Dad say you had tricked him. It was true, wasn't it?"
>
> Mom nodded. She was a long time answering. "Yes, that is true." (282–83)

Ironically, although Ellen lashes out at her mother with "I'm not like you," by the end of this scene, as Ellen starts to understand how compromise and complexity are truly the most basic elements of love, she in fact becomes closer to and more like her mother—and considerably less romantic (and potentially vulnerable) because of her mother's reaction to this outpouring.

Throughout the novel, the winter wheat has been metaphorically analogous to the love between Ellen's parents and the family's difficult existence. The narrator's depiction of winter wheat cultivation is far-removed from any romanticized version of agriculture as a pastoral idyll, just as Ben and Anna's marriage is not a romanticized picture of happiness. The dry, un-irrigated land used for these crops is of the poorest agricultural quality. In a business already riddled with uncertainties of weather, disease, and the marketplace, winter wheat farmers are highly exposed to failure and their livelihoods are constantly compromised. Walker demonstrates that the business of winter wheat farming, like its farmers' lives, is utterly unromantic.

Modernist Walker relies on this reality to explore the nature of love. When they met, Ben was a crippled soldier far from home, and Anna was a lonely teenager, eager to escape from the losses and horrors of war. Their lives were less than they had planned. Together, they forged a union. Unwelcome as a couple of a mixed marriage in Ben's Puritan New England home, the two chose a life on those hard dry plains of Montana. Through its narrator, *Winter Wheat* asks if the two were brought together by love or desperation. The novel concludes with the notion that desperation and the human desire to survive may, in fact, be the most genuine seeds of love. Anna reinforces this implication when Walker writes: "Mom picked up her whitewash brush and slapped it against the rough boards. "*Yólochka*, you don't know how love is yet" (284). In hearing these words and in her subsequent reconciliation with her mother, Ellen comes to a greater understanding of both her own femininity and her mother's.

Winter Wheat ends with the possibility that Ellen might eventually marry Warren, a widower. Such a marriage is a far cry from a young girl's romanticized version of love; instead, it too would be a compromise between highly romantic expectations and harsh reality. With this novel, Walker, unlike some modernists who have an antagonism toward the possibility of love, maintains a space for love's existence but not for its romanticized version. As such, Anna Webb in *Winter Wheat* is one of Walker's best examples of a mother with modernist leanings.

The mothers in many of Walker's other novels are also often

representative of the old world and order and are symbolic of a fractured, traditional world that no longer functions effectively in modern times. This is the case in *Fireweed*. Celie Henderson's mother grows old prematurely, cooking and maintaining a boarding house for mill workers. She is portrayed as a reticent Scandinavian immigrant who dies at an early age from hard work. Young Celie does not wish to choose her mother as a role model. Instead she looks for role models in figures from the cinema and popular magazines. She does not wear the home-sewn cotton dresses worn by her mother and other working women in Big Bay. Instead, she orders fine and often impractical clothes from mail-order catalogs. Celie yearns to leave the Upper Peninsula and begin a more rewarding and glamorous life in a bigger town far from her birthplace and constantly struggles with fears of growing old and worn down like her mother. In fact, Celie's adolescent impulses emerge from a rejection of her mother and her mother's way of living. However, as the novel progresses, Celie matures and comes to reconcile her life with that of her mother's.

For instance after a visit with friends who have moved to a bigger town, Celie considers their cramped living conditions and the scarcity and compromises they must make for their new lives and begins to see her own existence and that of her parents in a different light. By the end of the novel, Celie begins to take on some of her mother's mannerisms, but out of choice, not habit. For instance, as Celie considers her future in this remote part of Michigan, the narrator writes:

> Whatever fears Celie had for the future, she shut her lips tightly upon, like Christina [her mother] [. . .]. She would always have to work hard; there would be more babies and she would look tired the way Christina did, but it didn't matter so much.
>
> Rosie and Joe [their children] would go away. She would bring them up with that idea. They'd make a success across the straits and come back and wonder how she ever stood it up here. It was all right; plenty of things were left to her,

> after all; seeing Rosie and Jolie grow up and make their way, watching Joe leave the house and come back, his head thrown back a little and his arms swinging so loose, the way they did, from his shoulders; knowing him better every year, his body and his thoughts even when he didn't talk, and his words. (313)

The implication in this passage is that although Celie will not escape the convention and life that she associates with her mother, she has matured and is beginning to appreciate her mother's values and choice of lifestyle. As Celie begins to view her existence with a more mature eye, she finds a luminescence in the fireweed and in her husband's simple movements and is warmed by the thoughts of her growing intimacy with him. Even though, on the surface, she has not escaped a life similar to that of her mother's, she has, in fact, chosen this particular way of life rather than having it thrust upon her, and that makes all the difference. The implication here is that Celie realizes that her immigrant parents made a similarly independent choice years earlier and dignified their lives with their own unique expressions of freedom and self-creation.

Light from Arcturus once again paints a picture of the young woman moving away from her mother. In this case, the portrayal is considerably more Jamesian, and especially reminiscent of Henry James's novel *The Golden Bowl*. James's character Charlotte Stuart marries millionaire American Adam Verver and is initially happy enough to travel around with him in Europe as he builds his art collection for a museum he intends to leave as his legacy for the American people. However, when Charlotte finally realizes that the end-product of this journey is to return to America and present this culture to the American working people, she is horrified by the prospect of returning to live in what she sees as an uncultured society. Similarly, *Light from Arcturus* presents a young American woman who must reconcile her desire for culture with her destiny to live within what she sees as the uncultured heartland of America. At the start of the novel, the young Julia Hauser departs physically from her cultured, European-born family living in Chicago to marry a good-hearted but somewhat boring and inartistic businessman. Together, they move to a quiet, safe, and prosperous town in the Midwest. In this novel, the daughter does not purposely reject her mother. Instead, it is implicit in the text that it is this young woman's destiny to make a life apart from her own immigrant family and mother by marrying into an old American family and becoming assimilated into that life. In fact, Walker characterizes Julia as orphan-like in this new life. Although her family lives in Chicago for much of the novel, she rarely communicates with them; then, when she finally decides to leave the stultifying Midwest town to return to Chicago to visit (or perhaps stay) with her parents, she is thwarted in this reunion by their untimely and permanent return to Europe. Julia Hauser's dilemma is then to reconcile her destiny by compromising her desires and needs alongside those of her husband and children. These reconciliations include the necessity for her to flourish in "a man's world" and for her to create a plan to supplement the thwarted provincial education of their children. In Julia's mind, her children's fulfillment demands the stimulation of artistic and creative thought represented by such events as the Philadelphia Centennial Exposition of 1876 and the Chicago World's Fair of 1893.

One of the biggest sacrifices that Julia suffers in her marriage is the loss of her maternal connections that she intuitively senses she needs to make her life complete. Even from the beginning of her marriage, these sacrifices create a narrative tension that builds as the novel progresses. For instance, upon arrival in her new hometown of Halstead, Julia and her husband live in the town's hotel until their home is built. On the first day, when Julia leaves her room and goes down to the lobby, she is uncomfortably surrounded only by men and thinks to herself that "it was clearly a man's world" (31). Later, when she visits with the other women of the town, she discovers that some of them share her ambivalent feelings about life in Halstead. For instance, on her initial visit with Faith, a young woman like herself who has arrived a few years earlier, Julia is startled when she asks, "Do you like it here?" and is then told, "Oh, it's a good country for the men. It has a future perhaps we'll all be rich some day . . . but I . . . I paint, and I wish sometimes that I could just see some paintings, real ones, and talk with people about painting again. [. . .] I believe I hate it here" (36). However, despite the fact that, from early on in her years in Halstead, Julia becomes aware that she is not alone in how she feels, this knowledge does not connect her with these individuals—nor does it comfort her.

Walker compares Julia's artistic sensibility and frustrated sense of incompleteness to male characters as well as to selected females. For instance, Dr. Chapman is depicted as a misplaced British doctor who loathes the uncultured life he must live in Halstead. Even Julia's own husband occasionally mentions that he misses the music from the East Coast. But all these characters forego their aesthetic longings in order to advance the community's commercial prosperity. As they follow Julia through the early days of her marriage and motherhood, readers of *Light from Arcturus* repeatedly learn that she is not at all unique in her hunger and alienation and that her struggles are representative of the community's.

Lifelines to Julia's mother filter through the text like the shimmering light from Arcturus. In one particularly poignant scene, Julia is alone and cold in a hotel room as she listens to the men playing cards downstairs and to the wind howling in from across the prairie. She cannot sleep and opens her trunk to rummage through her things from home and finds a book her mother had given her, *The Family Physician*. Alone in her room, her icy hands turn the pages to "Pregnancy." This seventeen-year-old then reads the descriptions in the text and shyly examines her body for signs. She reads through the section titled "Labor" and returns to her covers, feeling small and alone. Somehow, the text is a link to her mother and her grandmother, the only physical connection that remains. Wisely, her mother sensed that her daughter would need this in her new life and slipped the book into Julia's wedding trunk, advising: "You can't tell about Doctors way out there, Julia, and it's nice to look up things for yourself. You're a married woman now and you should know things" (60–61). Perhaps beyond these practical concerns, Julia's mother also recognized the inevitable challenges her daughter would face. As the marriage progresses, Julia thinks to herself, "Her body was making itself into Max's wife, but she always had a feeling of not quite being one with him. It was all mixed up; she couldn't think [. . .] if only Max could understand how she felt!" (52) Throughout the novel, despite her mixed feelings, Julia raises their children and supports her family, her husband's business, and the community, while secretly maintaining a long-term focus and determination to return and reconnect with the bright lights and artistic vigor of the city, which she succeeds in finding. By the final chapters of *Light from Arcturus* Julia's family has moved to Chicago and enjoys Julia's long-sought cultured life. Despite this fulfillment, however, the author once again carefully inserts enough details for readers to understand that there is yet another compromise and sacrifice in this choice of lifestyle. In order to create a space for the "female-gendered," artistic side of the family unit, some of the rational and pragmatic aspects of the family's previous life have to be surrendered. Hence, the family resides in Chicago without many of their earlier material and economic comforts, and the alterations of the traditional perspectives on gender in the family unit require compromises on everyone's part. This is apparent by the fact that the men in the family suffer more than the women. Julia's son, in fact, rejects his new life in Chicago and announces to his mother that he will be returning to a small Midwestern town to open a business similar to his father's.

As an epilogue, the author includes a final chapter, set over thirty years after the family's move to Chicago, titled "The Bird of Time—1933." In this chapter, the narrator portrays Julia Hauser at seventy-four. In this chapter Julia flies to Chicago to visit one more World's Fair. By this time, her children are scattered across the country and busy with their own lives and are not particularly interested in World Fairs, but some of them attend it with her with what Julia interprets as almost as a gratuitous humoring. As she sits on the plane returning home, remembering the choices she made in her life and its consequences on her family, she contemplates:

> They [her children] had forgotten how hard she had struggled to get to the last Fair. Of course the children didn't think much of the Fair. People didn't need Fairs now, they had radios and moving-pictures; they weren't isolated, that was it.
>
> Going away now wasn't like leaving that first Fair in Philadelphia when she had felt she was leaving everything, going into a kind of exile. Max [her husband] had seemed almost like a stranger; everything ahead was unknown. And then they had gotten there and Halstead [Nebraska] was worse than she had feared, not even dangerous nor rough, just cramped, already set in narrow rut. She had tried to live there. But she couldn't have the children grow up there. Max never wanted to leave. Even now she was sorry because of Max; even taking care of him all those years hadn't made it up to him, but Max hadn't blamed her. Maybe Max understood [. . .]. (343)

This final passage of the novel again demonstrates the author's sensitivity in handling both her male and female characters and her complex notion of gender. Because the narrative has Julia ponder the question of whether Max ever understood her needs, the text again demonstrates a male sensitivity to the many requirements brought on by a modern sense of gender.

It is noteworthy that Julia chooses this same word "understand" at both the beginning and end of the novel. At the start, Julia wishes, "If only Max understood" and then returns to this word at the end by speculating, "Maybe Max understood." Believing that he "understood" allows Julia to accept that he had potentially reconciled his own discordant and engendered needs.

Ironically, *Light from Arcturus* ends with a presentation of yet the next generational rift between mothers and daughters. By this point, the elderly version of the protagonist, Julia Hauser, has become representative of the outdated values and traditional mother-figures of an earlier era, and readers sense that her own daughters seek to escape from this mother image. At the end of the novel, Julia Hauser, now a mother figure herself, flies away from her daughters. Readers leave this story with a sense of the cyclical nature of this mother-daughter struggle.

One of the most troubling mother-daughter relationships in Walker's novels appears in *The Curlew's Cry*. Pamela Lacey's relationship with her mother is perpetually fraught with conflict. In fact, one might say that Pamela's early rejection of her husband and marriage, which her mother encouraged and created, can be read as Pamela's rebellion against her mother's values. Perhaps because Pamela, more so than any other female character of Walker's, outwardly rejects her mother, she is also the character who most often finds the need to seek out an alternative maternal figure as a replacement.

From the opening pages of *The Curlew's Cry* readers witness Pamela Lacey's free spirit and sense of rebellion. When, for example, her teacher asks the class for suggestions for a float in the Pioneer Days parade and the boys suggest the usual vigilante theme, it is Pamela who raises her slender arm and politely suggests that the float be divided in two, one half for the boys' vigilante drama and the other for a creation inspired by the girls. Pamela is disappointed, however, when the female side of the float is nothing more than an adjunct to the drama on the boys' side, presenting the stereotypical image of women weeping over their lost men. For Pamela, the worst thing about this choice is that it emerges from the females in the class. Because of the inability of the females around her to escape from their roles vis-à-vis the men, Pamela is attracted to the company of men. In men, she senses an independence that the women, especially her mother, seem to lack. One example of this appears in a scene when her father's business associates come to the house for a dinner and talk. As Pamela leans forward to listen to the men, her mother whispers and chides her to stop leaning so forward in her chair and to stop looking so interested. In frustration, Pamela thinks:

> Why didn't Mama listen to what they were saying instead of being so busy watching everything? [. . .]
>
> Mama's eyes and mouth moved together in an expression that said, "You and I are ladies and must keep our minds on certain things." Pamela sat up straighter but she turned her eye back to her father. (24)

Later in the novel, when Pamela graduates from school and is confronted with planning her future, her mother encourages a marriage with the son of a wealthy business associate. Faced with few other alternatives, her father's economic and spiritual collapse, the underlying pressing needs of the business arrangement of the marriage, and her mother's unrelenting desire for it, Pamela reluctantly marries. Not surprisingly, shortly into her somewhat compromised and commodified marriage, Pamela returns to the town of Brandon Rapids for a visit and surprises everyone by remaining there permanently, announcing her divorce from her husband. In the East, not only did Pamela feel confined by the house and the walled gardens, but also by the rigid conventions of men and women's roles. (For a more detailed analysis of this economic aspect of marriage in the West and "the objectification and commodificat[ion]" of women and female authors' reaction to this, see Victoria Lamont's essay "Cattle Branding and the Traffic in Women in Early Twentieth-Century Westerns by Women" in *Legacy* [30].) Sensing that her freedom might be more easily achieved in the West, Pamela embarks on a new life as a divorced woman. This life is also fraught with its own set of difficulties. Now a threatening figure to many of the town's women, Pamela is perceived as a divorced woman on the loose. Her status in the town is further eroded when her father's business practices are questioned and he loses most of his remaining interest in the family cattle operation. Throughout this period, Pamela becomes more estranged from her mother. Her mother despairs at their growing separation, claiming not to understand her daughter at all. With this escalating estrangement, Pamela seeks a replacement for her mother in several members of her community. Not surprisingly, all of them are somewhat marginalized from the formal society of prominent women in Brandon Rapids, Montana. For example, during her schoolgirl days, Pamela befriends Rose Guinard. Rose is the daughter of a French immigrant mother and milliner, Madame Guinard, who has recently settled in Brandon Falls. Without a husband, Madame Guinard's very home embodies the family's marginalized status as a single-parent household. It is tucked up on a side street, above the milliner's shop, out of sight from the townspeople. Predictably, Pamela's mother questions her friendship with these "foreign sorts." However, Pamela continues in this company and knows better than to let her mother learn that most of Madame Guinard's income is derived from making hats for the women from the house of ill-repute, who are, ironically, paid by the community's upstanding male citizens. It appears that Rose and her mother's unconventionality are exactly what initially attract Pamela to them. For instance, when Rose announces that she will ask a boy to the school dance, Pamela responds with shock:

> "Oh, you couldn't, Rose!" Pamela said seriously and then stopped as Rose laughed.
>
> "Just for fun I'd like to try. I'd ask Wrenn to take me. His mother was in the shop the other day and said he'd be home this week."
>
> Pamela puzzled over Rose as she went down the street. You couldn't ask a boy to take you to a dance, that was the trouble with being a girl. (95)

Despite this unconventionality, Pamela and Rose become good friends, and their schoolgirl friendship is characterized by its intimacy. When the girls stay at the ranch, they share a bed, their stories, and their dreams and wrap their arms around each other as they sleep. However, this intimacy is lost when Rose marries Wrenn and her status is subsequently elevated to membership with the respectable and leading women in the community. As this occurs, Rose's friendship with Pamela is nearly severed. In Pamela's mind, their parting of ways is inevitable because she had always thought she might marry Wrenn herself, and this misconception haunts Pamela throughout the text, causing a number of misunderstandings—of which her estranged friendship is but one result. But even when Pamela loses Rose as her childhood friend, she maintains the close relationship she had previously established with Rose's mother. As an outsider to the community, and as a single, successful, and independent businesswoman, Madame Guinard is a role model as Pamela grows into her own hard-fought independence.

Another older female character, Ruby, the ranch cook and solitary female in the all-male environment of the family ranch, is Pamela's closest mother figure throughout the novel. Ruby has lived most of her life in a man's world, as a camp cook on cattle drives and at various ranches. She is wiry and dresses like the cowhands around her. With a cigarette in her mouth, punctuated by coarse language, Ruby maintains a utilitarian and what might be characterized as a masculine household out at the ranch—with hot coffee, a warm fire, overflowing ashtrays, and linens on the beds from last month. Not surprisingly, Pamela's friendship with Ruby also worries Pamela's mother. In fact, it worries her so much that she repeatedly questions her husband about the wisdom of Pamela spending so much time with Ruby. However, Pamela ignores her mother and finds in Ruby's clipped and coarse language an articulation of concerns that she cannot find elsewhere. When, for instance, Pamela finds herself alone and panicking after Alan is bitten by a rattlesnake on the ranch, it is her memory of Ruby's words that guides her as she prepares to cut an "X" on the bite to suck the venom from his arm: "It's all foolishness that a girl can't stick a chicken in the throat; men are twice as squeamish as women any day" (57). Then, when Pamela forges ahead with her marriage plans to Alan, despite her own misgivings, it is again Ruby who admonishes her and articulates Pamela's feelings.

> "I bet your mother goes for him."
>
> "Yes, she likes him."
>
> Ruby gave a snort [. . .] [and] pulled the quilts up over Pamela's shoulder. "Take your time, Pam, don't go rushing off." Ruby's voice could be low sometimes and as comfortable as warmth. (171)

Then, when Pamela returns to the ranch as a divorced woman, it is Ruby, seemingly struggling and irritated with her own marriage to an often drunken hired ranch hand, who again puts words to the source of Pamela's troubles. As Pamela looks wistfully out the window of the ranch house upon her arrival from the East, Ruby observes:

> "You miss queer things when you ain't happy [. . .] so that professor of yours let you come west for a change!"
>
> "Well, I came anyway, Ruby." [. . .]
>
> "Did you leave him for good?" she asked, yellow-gray eyes almost crossed as she looked at the cigarette paper she was sealing with her tongue.
>
> "I don't know yet." Pamela took off her hat and jacket.
>
> "Do you love the lady cowboy [Alan]?" Ruby lighted a match with her fingernail.
>
> "I didn't ever really love him," Pamela said, her eyes on the slow movement of the river.
>
> "That's the worst thing a women can do, Punk. It makes me ashamed of myself that I never taught you any better. It's worse than a lot of things people think is worse. Unless you both know it and then it ain't right." (230)

After this admonishment, Pamela retreats from the ranch, from Ruby, and from society in general to reevaluate her own actions. After a period of estrangement, the two are reunited when Ruby's husband dies in World War I. In this scene, the older woman again teaches a still lost and struggling Pamela something about love and fulfillment. Despite Ruby's apparent harshness and lack of femininity, she breaks down with her husband's death. In this scene, Pamela has the opportunity to finally reach out to a mother figure, but even while witnessing this tender and moving event, she is still confused and does not accept her own tender inclinations:

> Ruby had wanted to go right back [to the ranch] after Slim's funeral.
>
> "You don't think I want to stay in that woman's town, do you?" Ruby had asked as they drove toward the ranch. [. . .]
>
> Once Ruby had burst out, "Damn fool to go off to the army in the first place. I told him he'd get killed." [. . .]
>
> [Pamela] had been ashamed that she was so glad to get away [. . .]. She had tried to think of something to say to Ruby, or tried to touch out to comfort her. Women comforted each other with their arms, but she couldn't seem to do it, she stood there going on with her own thoughts. Then she looked at Ruby and saw tears on her face. It was so terrible to see Ruby cry she put her arms around her.
>
> "You loved Slim; you never married him without."
>
> Ruby had sniffed hard. "You're damned right, Punk, but a women's a fool to love a man like I did that one." She put another stick on the stove and clattered the teakettle back over. "Might as well cook onions tonight; I'm bound to snivel anyways." (284)

In this scene, despite Ruby's tough veneer, her deep expression of need for another's love and her own complex interpretation of gender are apparent. Although Ruby admits that she cannot wait to get out of that "woman's town," she by no means attempts to escape from her own tender and "womanly side." Pamela makes an effort in this scene to demonstrate her emotional tenderness toward Ruby, but her actions are inhibited and she fails to make the connection. Once again, after this event,

Pamela retreats into her world of business and men, denying and ignoring many of her own needs. But, in this solitary time, Pamela begins to transform and, in her own way, reconcile with a "return to the mother." Slowly, she works to make the ranch more feminine and homely, filling the cabins with western décor. Here, readers sense aspects of the domesticity that Pamela has learned from her mother and other women. But it is only after the death of Pamela's mother and Ruby's departure to marry again and start a new life that Pamela is finally forced to confront the full crisis caused by denying her own gendered needs, needs that she has tried to ignore her entire life. In fact, at this point in the novel, with both her mother and father dead and Ruby gone, almost all the individuals in her life who to her represented the gendered binary—male or female—are gone.

Alone, Pamela realizes she has proven to herself that she can succeed in business in a man's world and that the independence she has long associated with the male world is not the entire answer to her personal fulfillment. She turns back to her long-estranged and now widowed childhood friend, Rose. The novel ends with Pamela's invitation to Rose to come and live out at the ranch. As *The Curlew's Cry* ends, Pamela finally utters words that she has considered analogous with weakness all her life: "'Rose, I've been very lonely out at the ranch this winter . . .'" (382). In these final lines, readers sense Pamela's ultimate success and reconciliation with a mother-figure and with her own full-bodied sense of self.

This substitution of another female representative of the original mother also occurs in *The Body of a Young Man* and *The Orange Tree*. In approaching the either / or and male / female binaries, these texts utilize two female protagonists whose diametrically opposed personalities and perceptions share the narrative. Although it is tempting to refer to this use of two females as an authorial attempt at presenting doppelgangers, there is a danger in doing so because, though one figure complements the other and often appears as its opposite, a composite of the qualities of both female figures would not necessarily create the completeness that characterizes doppelgangers. Instead, what occurs in these novels is a fusion and synergistic transformation of the qualities of both characters.

For instance, in *The Body of a Young Man*, Phyllis Cutler calls her husband's childhood friends under the premises that she cannot cope or help him with his grief and guilt resulting from the suicide of one of his high school students and that perhaps they might be able to help him. Her husband's old friends, Lucy and Josh Blair, then generously invite Phyllis, Jim, and their son to share the summer with them in their guest house at their property in Vermont. Throughout the novel, Phyllis is outwardly obsessed with helping her husband out of his depression, and her worries over this dominate all other matters. However, a closer examination of the text reveals the fact that Jim's problems are a dramatic aside to the novel's true tension, as is the young man's suicide. In fact, Jim, Phyllis's husband, hardly ever speaks throughout the novel and is a shadowy and quiet figure who rarely asks for anything and is resentful when others thrust their well-meaning opinions on him. Readers soon learn that it is Phyllis who is truly the needy one and who continues to seek advice from her friends with her nervous energy and soulful glances. The discovery of her gnawing need (characterized, symbolically, by the gnawing of the raccoon in a cage that the children bring up to the porch) is central to the novel.

Although readers learn nothing about Jim's background, they do learn that Phyllis somehow associates the distancing she senses from her own husband with the separation she felt as a child when her parents divorced. At one point, she even suggests to Lucy that her overwrought nature might be brought on by being the by-product of a divorced family. "I wonder if all children of divorced parents sound as I do or whether I'm neurotic." Lucy responds with, "Jim adores you," somehow sensing that what is at the crux of Phyllis's worries is some feeling of rejection and repeated victimization. Phyllis is so caught up in her own drama that even when Lucy and Josh put music on their record player, she does not enjoy the tunes. Instead, she remembers the lonely music her mother constantly played as they sat in the apartment after her husband left her for another woman. Phyllis, although she doesn't realize it, resents her mother's weakness during those years and also resents and fears her mother's inability to have done anything more than react to her situation. Phyllis intuitively senses and fears that she is also at risk of becoming her mother and of being caught in a similar trap. Her mother reacted as a victimized woman and was entrapped in what some might call the traditional patriarchal social order, being the reactive female rather than the proactive male. Phyllis's mother died without ever having moved on, and whether or not Phyllis realizes it, deep down it is her own sense of being caught in a similarly proscribed identity that she fears most, somehow believing that her mother was and will always be her sole role model.

In Lucy, Phyllis finds a very different female role model from her mother. Although Lucy is sensuous and domestic, a loving mother, wife, and hostess, and is very feminine, she is also self-centered, strong, and understands the importance of a woman having "a room of her own." In Lucy's case, the room is a small area in the barn where she goes each day to weave. Her weaving is very personal. It is time spent away from family and community needs. It is this going away that gives Lucy a sense of centering, strength, and self-confidence that Phyllis lacks. Although Phyllis senses this and Lucy makes overtures to reach out to her, Phyllis rejects these overtures. For instance, when the women are alone, Phyllis constantly steers the conversation back to her husband, as though sensing that his existence and identity are her own. Intuitively, Lucy understands the danger in this misconception and encourages Phyllis to discuss her own needs, but Phyllis continues to retreat into discussions solely concerning her husband's work and worries. Even when the women go off for a weekend to a weaving show, Phyllis rejects

Lucy's reaching out. This is most apparent when the women find that the only accommodation in the busy village is a single room in a hotel where they must share a bed. As naturally as she would hug her children or kiss her husband, Lucy reaches out to Phyllis to give her a warm kiss and embrace after the women finish talking about Jim and his troubles:

> Lucy's voice was warm. "Phyl, how can I make you understand that Josh and I love you both. The idea of giving up anything [helping you this summer] doesn't enter the picture at all." She leaned over and kissed Phyllis. "Don't be foolish." Then she turned over, arranging her pillow noisily.
>
> Phyllis turned on her side, moving a little closer to the outside. Lucy's words were comforting, but the sudden kiss embarrassed her. She couldn't find anything to say, and she was unsure of her own voice. She needn't be uncomfortable, or apologetic. "Josh and I love you both . . ." Lucy had said. It was so amazing.
>
> The silence grew softly in the room. She wished the room were dark, not half dark like this. She felt strange sleeping with Lucy . . . as though the awareness in their bodies of lying, Lucy with Josh, she with James, made them secretive or shy. No . . . that wasn't what separated them and made their talk dwindle into an uneasy silence. It was—wasn't it?—that they were not quite comfortable with each other because their minds held secret things Josh and James had said? [. . .] Their minds were secret and turned away. (110)

In this scene of potential intimacy, Phyllis and Lucy both turn from each other. Despite Lucy's natural and warm embrace, Phyllis once again tries to subsume her own identity and Lucy's within the boundaries of their husbands' identities. She tries to convince herself that they are uncomfortable solely because of the secrets that each of them shares with their respective husbands. However, a reader is left to wonder if Phyllis turns away because there is in fact something else that both women share. Ann Ardis comments on this matter in *New Women, New Novels*. In discussing some women-centered texts, she writes: "Equally significant, the bonding between women figured in these novels is homoerotic without being lesbian in the conventional sense of that term" (138). Ardis's use of "homoerotic" may be a troublesome term here because its popular use seems to imply a physical sexual involvement, but Ardis attempts to carefully distinguish homoeroticism from lesbianism. What is relevant in Ardis's discussion relative to this scene is that there can be deep feelings between individuals of the same sex without any implications of physicality and that, in fact, the fulfillment of these needs contributes to a fuller sense of self.

Given all this underlying tension and drama, the dénouement of *The Body of a Young Man* occurs, not surprisingly, not when Jim has made some peace with his involvement with his student's suicide but when Phyllis comes to a greater awareness of herself and her own complex identity and needs, quite apart from the needs of her husband. As the two women reflect back on their time together during the summer, Phyllis finally begins to understand the root of her own insecurities while responding to Lucy with a refreshing lucidity and forceful confidence.

> "As time goes on, Jim will get the whole miserable memory out of his mind, don't you think?" Lucy says.
>
> "No, [. . .]. Some things, if they hurt enough, are always going to be buried in your mind, I think, so that all your thoughts have to [. . .] grow out of their dust." (157)

It is from this point that Phyllis begins to heal by reconciling with her past and her seemingly divergent needs, gendered in both the traditional binary conceptions of masculine and feminine. Part of the "dust" she refers to is the residual influence of her mother and the legacy that her mother's life has imparted on her own. Phyllis finally understands that her past, her needs, and her insecurities are nothing to be ashamed of. Furthermore, she realizes that the real danger in her life is ignoring or attempting to suppress her ambivalent feelings about her mother and her own lingering fears of again becoming the victimized woman. Although her mother is dead, at the end of the novel Phyllis makes peace with her mother and her legacy and is able to move on with a more confident and fuller sense of self.

Another example of Walker's young female characters' complex relationships and subsequent growth due to the mother figure appears in *The Brewers' Big Horses*. In this novel, Sara Henkel's mother is ineffective in assisting her daughter in a world where Victorian tastes and sensibilities are no longer the ideal. This mother figure is similar to many Jamesian mothers (such as *Daisy Miller*), and a reader can sympathize easily with Sara's desire to join the male world rather than remain in her mother's limited and outdated "feminine space." In *The Brewers' Big Horses*, Sara Henkel's only sympathetic friends and mentors during the years of her struggles in business are the old German gentlemen at the brewery. However, when Prohibition comes and the brewery faces bankruptcy, Sara Henkel also falls back on her feminine guiles, cleverly opening a "beer-less beer garden" with music and tea to help the business survive the dry years. This is creative problem-solving based primarily on the skills she learned from her mother and other women and a way of life she had earlier rejected. Walker's message is clear: success requires a blending and synergistic re-creation of both the hardened acumen traditionally attributed to the male and the innovative and intuitive creativity most often associated with the female.

Throughout her novels, Walker attempts to demonstrate that these inclinations and traditional characterizations are not exclusively the terrains of neither males nor females. In fact, in all her novels, both male and female characters grapple with questions of gender and struggle for fulfillment through an escape from the traditional, binary roles they find themselves caught within. Her characters' efforts to escape from these binaries and, in the case of the women, return to the mother figures show them coming to terms with the freedoms and challenges of modernist thought.

7. American Modernists and the Language of Movement

There is no doubt that modern life can be characterized by words such as "change," "movement," and "speed." The development in the twentieth century of more efficient machines—of faster trains, automobiles, and planes—helped a rural society transform into a more urban and fast-paced culture. The reaction of the public and its writers to these dynamic changes was varied and complex. (For more detailed discussions on movement, machinery, and America, see *Shifting Gears: Technology, Literature, Culture in Modernist America* by Cecilia Tichi and *Civilizing the Machine: Technology and Republican Values in America 1776–1900* by John F. Kasson.) For instance, modernists who referred to themselves as futurists embraced this new fast and exciting world. Other groups and individuals lamented these changes, citing the erosion of a slower (and often better) way of life and the values associated with that lifestyle. However, most individuals, writers and artists included, sat somewhere in the middle, both fascinated and frightened by the rapidity of change and its far-reaching effects. Perhaps no writer better expressed this feeling than Henry Adams in his chapter "The Virgin and the Dynamo" from *The Education of Henry Adams*. Many modernist writers who followed in Adams's steps were similarly inclined: both mesmerized and elated by these changes, and, at other times, distraught by the erosion that rapid industrialization brought to traditional American society. Whether individuals were intrigued by, embraced, rejected, or tacitly observed these rapid changes, however, all modernists were both touched and changed irrevocably by the dynamic times in which they lived.

On this subject, Gertrude Stein, in a speech entitled "How Writing is Written," claimed that:

> In the Twentieth Century you [Americans] feel like movement. The Nineteenth Century didn't feel that way. The element of movement was not the predominating thing that they felt. You know that in your lives movement is the thing that occupies you most—you feel movement all the time. And the United States had the first instance of what I call Twentieth Century writing. You see it first in Walt Whitman. He was the beginning of the movement. He didn't see it very clearly, but there was a sense of movement that the European was very much influenced by, because the Twentieth Century became the American Century. That is what I mean when I say that each generation has its own literature. (qtd. in Scott, *Gender of Modernism* 489–90)

Stein makes several interesting points here, the primary one being that movement certainly can be said to characterize the twentieth century as well as modernist writing both in its subject matter and style. In the twentieth century in particular, movement and literature came together in a way they never had before, accelerating and defining that fundamental characterization of Americans as a people of movement, displacement, and self-invention.

Stein's mention of Walt Whitman brings to mind his *Song of Myself*, in which he celebrates the vibrancy of American life in the streets of New York in the mid-nineteenth century. This vibrant quality owes not only to physical movement and activity but also to what Whitman perceived as America's indigenous mobility and dynamism. For Whitman, the road and the movement of its people exemplified the American spirit. Similarly, Mark Twain's Huck Finn, the quintessential American boy, is characterized by his movement. In perhaps the most famous lines of Twain's novel, the boy states, "But I reckon I got to light out for the Territory ahead of the rest, because Aunt Sally she's going to adopt me and sivilize [sic] me and I can't stand it. I been there before" (Twain 320). These lines are noteworthy for several reasons. First, they capture the restlessness of the American spirit. Second, they indicate, to a certain extent, the sense of rootlessness and homelessness and the necessity for self-invention felt by the early modern American. And third, they illustrate what Stein refers to when she says, "You know that in your lives movement is the thing that occupies you most—you feel movement all the time."

For many modernist American writers, rootlessness, restlessness, and self-invention dominated both their lives and their prose. Writers such as Hemingway and Fitzgerald come to mind, moving their families from one place to another, shifting with the seasons and their varying dispositions from the north to the south, from one country to another. Similarly, their fictional characters were constantly on the move. The automobile that Stein refers to also plays a role in their novels. Some of the best examples of this are found in the many scenes with automobiles featured in *The Great Gatsby*. Nick Carraway, the narrator of the novel, uses Gatsby's car to characterize its owner and America: "He was balancing himself on the running board of his car with that resourcefulness of movement that is so peculiarly American—that comes, I suppose, with the absence of lifting work or rigid sitting in youth and, even more, with the formless grace of our nervous, sporadic games" (59).

Even Mildred Walker, born into a seemingly staid family that had settled in the Massachusetts Bay Colony in the 1630s and had lived for centuries in New England (Hugo 11), entered into a life of continuous movement. In her childhood, because of her father's work as a Baptist minister, her family moved numerous times from, in Walker's words, "one poorly appointed parsonage to another" (qtd. in Hugo: 30). By the time she graduated from high school, she had attended four schools in four years (Hugo 43). Coupled with this movement was the family's annual exodus from Philadelphia and its outlying communities to their summer home in Grafton, Vermont. In those days, the annual trip required a train, a seafaring ship, and, in its last leg into the Vermont hills, a horse and buggy. After marrying Ferdinand Schemm, Walker's life of movement accelerated. She found herself moving to a logging camp in Northern Michigan, which was followed by a year in England, a return to Michigan, and then a move out to Montana. After her husband's death she returned to her alma mater in upstate New York and then, in her retirement, lived in Vermont, Montana, and Oregon. Walker even moved one more time after her death, back to Saginaw, Michigan, to be buried alongside her husband's grave. These major household moves during her lifetime were complemented by numerous trips over the years. These included a year abroad in Japan, a winter in Sicily, and numerous journeys throughout the United States and Europe. Like her contemporaries, Walker was born into a century of movement. Today, her three children are scattered across the country in the Pacific Northwest, the Rocky Mountains, and New England. Her grandchildren are scattered across the globe, some living in Europe and the Middle East. In the globalized twenty-first century, movement continues for her offspring and for many Americans on an increasingly broader scale.

Personally, Walker both lamented and embraced this movement. In *Writing for Her Life*, Ripley Hugo indicates that as a girl, her mother felt in many ways inferior to the people around her who had more settled lives and positions. However, Hugo also indicates that when her mother and father moved to a remote logging town in Upper Michigan, Mildred made it clear to everyone around her that she was not there to stay but, at the same time, also secretly admitted that she enjoyed the move and the temporary feeling of being a pioneer of sorts. Again, when Walker and her family first arrived in Montana, a state that would not have been her mother's first choice for a home, Ripley Hugo again points to evidence of her mother's feelings of alienation with the world around her in both the entries in her journals and in the fact that she wrote about Montana from an outsider's perspective for many years before she felt she could inhabit artistically that landscape with a fictional character of her own creation. As further evidence of her mother's ambivalence, Hugo quotes from cards for a speech her mother gave in the 1960s that read: "Montana was so vast and strange to me that I didn't dare write about it for almost ten years, though I wrote about eastern dudes there in a novel called *Unless the Wind Turns*" (qtd. in Hugo:129).

Living in the twentieth-century world of change, displacement, invigoration, and alienation were never a reality Walker overlooked when she re-created American scenes in her fiction. In fact, it was very much a preoccupation with her characters and underlay the point of tension in many of her novels. Interestingly, in her first novel, readers might note that the narrator did not initially portray her characters with faces and bodies but instead only with feet. In fact, *Fireweed* begins with a description of the hobnailed boots tromping through the snow and mud in a small town on the Upper Peninsula. Its heroine has shoes and a gait different from the others. Celie Henderson's character is introduced only by her shoes, which are not from the local merchant but instead from a mail-order catalog. Although all the feet are moving, her distinctive feet are headed somewhere else. The opening scenes of the novel indicate that this narrative might be read as a study in frustrated movement. Its protagonist, Celie, senses and wants to be part of the vibrant changes occurring in U.S. society in the 1920s and 1930s, and this desire is both the source of the novel's tension and of Celie's characterization. In what might be considered the novel's dénouement, Celie and her husband are caught in a snowstorm in their old Ford. Frantically, Celie demands that they keep moving forward. Even when their car is high-ended on a snow bank, she and her husband attempt to continue their journey by walking along in the blizzard. As the couple is halted in their efforts by cold and fatigue, readers sense that in this scene, Celie matures and comes to realize the limitations of her own and her family's mobility.

Throughout her novels, Walker utilizes similar analogies with vehicles, either moving or stuck, to illustrate the inner lives of her characters and their outward circumstances. For instance, in *Winter Wheat*, Ellen's boyfriend, Gil, gets the farm truck stuck in the gumbo after a Montana storm. Only Ellen can dislodge the marooned truck, indicating to readers that the future is hers only when she takes charge of the wheel. Again, in *The Brewers' Big Horses*, Walker introduces her protagonist by illustrating her character's fascination with movement. Young Sara Bolster secretly slips out from the confines of her stultifying Victorian home to catch a glimpse of the giant horses pulling the brewery wagons through the streets of Detroit. In the novel's opening descriptions, the narrator writes: "Sara started counting the carriages that passed, but the intervals between were too long. She gave up walking back and forth and sat at the base of the sundial, leaning her chin on her hand [. . .]. Noise on the avenue jerked her head up instantly; a jingling of horses' bridles, the sound of the enormous clop-clop of hoofs, the heavier rolling thunder of the big wheels [. . .]" (4). Readers learn that the young girl loves to sneak out of her Victorian home to watch the movement and excitement in the streets. In this passage, readers are reminded of Whitman's exuberant descriptions of horses on the streets of New York in *Song of Myself*. In Walker's novel, when the brewery driver asks Sara if she would like a ride, despite the fact that she knows such activity is strictly forbidden by her mother, she climbs up onto the wagon. This brief scene gives readers a sense of Sara's character and of the direction of the novel. For this protagonist, the confines of the Victorian home and the dusty life and remnants of the nineteenth century are stultifying, and life and movement outside the family's door is liberating. Again, readers sense this when Sara visits her father's office and she looks out his long window at the moving river and feels a "sense of space, a feeling of adventure" (45).

Much like Dorothy Richardson's free-spirited heroines in the modernist classic *Pointed Rooves*, Sara Bolster delights in a somewhat forbidden bike ride. In *Pointed Rooves*, Richardson repeatedly used the bicycle as a metaphor for her characters' feminine liberation. For instance, in one scene from *The Tunnel*, two women go biking after dark—in their knickers—because the encumbrances of their required clothing prevent such freedom of movement (148). In Sara's case, although she remains in her traditional garb, her delight is heightened by both the exhilaration and liberation of knowing that she is the first girl in town to ride a bicycle. This scene is noteworthy because Sara's mastery of the bicycle is the first critical step for this young woman in establishing her independence outside the home. In fact, once she has ridden the bicycle, her heightened sense of independence and confidence prompt her to reject her mother's admonitions about what is and is not proper for a young woman to do, and she defies her mother's wishes and secures a job as a reporter for the local newspaper. Readers later learn that "Sara had bought the bicycle with her own earnings and was using it for reporting" (140).

Throughout the novel, Sara senses that movement is to be the source of her freedom, success, and happiness. In the scene of her first bike ride, readers learn that her childhood friend, Paul, comes home from his university for Thanksgiving with the first bicycle seen in Armitage City, and "[h]e taught Sara how to ride it within the safe confines of the back yard." However, that isn't enough for Sara. She insists upon moving out of her family's yard both physically and emotionally. Sara recklessly takes the bike and continues pedaling through the town until she smashes into her friend Anne's big snowball bush. Quickly, she picks herself up and wipes a scratch on Paul's bike with her handkerchief and immediately thinks to herself, "Paul must think she made a perfect ride" (60). Metaphorically, this scene foreshadows all the actions in the novel that will follow. Sara will get caught up in the speed and excitement of the early twentieth century. Many times, she will crash but lift herself back up, hoping no one has noticed.

Repeatedly, this novel links movement with its protagonist's growth. However, even in this early novel, written in the late 1930s, Walker balanced carefully the optimism of the century, with its exhilarating pace, alongside the realities of the price its people must pay for this speed. Ironically, the very same giant horses and powerful movement that initiated Sara into a life of motion also kill her young husband. When a keg rolls off a loading platform and spooks the Clydesdales, Sara watches in horror as her husband is trampled by their great hooves. In this incident readers get a glimpse of the author's modernist ambivalence over the issues of speed and mobility in the twentieth century. Even in *Fireweed*, readers might recall that after all is said and done, the heroine's family is not lured, as their neighbors and friends are, into the faster-moving life of the growing urban centers to the south but instead choose to remain behind and forge an alternate existence with a healthier and slower-paced lifestyle. Despite the twists and turns in both these novels, however, its author could not be labeled as reactionary, nostalgic, or the slightest bit sentimental toward the past.

Again, in *Light from Arcturus*, Walker chooses the Philadelphia Exposition of 1876 and the Chicago World's Fair of 1893 as symbols for the future and the increasing movement of the nation. It is no coincidence that the novel introduces its heroine, Julia Hauser, on the first day of her honeymoon at the Philadelphia Exposition. Julia is caught up in the possibilities of her future that she sees in the shining lights and buildings and associates the possibilities she senses at that exposition with her own adult life as she embarks on her first days of marriage. Throughout the novel, Julia's conception of who she will become, embodied in the spirit of that exposition, is constantly undermined and frustrated. Despite this, Sara never gives up the hope that she is meant to be part of all that she witnessed in her first days of married life. Repeatedly, Walker demonstrates Julia's determination to be a participant in the movement of the country. In the opening paragraphs of the novel, Walker writes, "Julia Hauser reached out to all that lay ahead. She wanted things to happen; that was the expectancy in her dark eyes. She had no fear that perhaps she would not be equal to them . . . that confidence was the secret of her poise. Now she was going to the Centennial Exposition on her wedding trip" (3).

The novel again characterizes Sara's spirit in a scene that occurs shortly after the couple's arrival in Philadelphia. After the first day of their visit to the exposition, when her husband goes downstairs to play poker in their hotel, Sara finds herself confined to and frustrated in her room, peering through the windows at the passersby. Boldly, she slips out of the hotel by herself: "She had never been out on the street alone at night before, never in her life. She felt daring and filled with a strange new excitement" (20). Sara will yearn to re-create this feeling of excitement that comes with being part of the street scene and movement of the city throughout her life. In this novel, the future, with all its movement and excitement, is characterized positively through the perspective of Julia Hauser.

However, once again in this novel its author tempers Julia's "all-American" enthusiasm for the future and movement by demonstrating that a certain degree of homelessness is the price that her characters will pay for their mobility. Although the Hausers' lives may have been a bit on the dull side throughout their years in Nebraska, they were enriched with close friendships and a sense of belonging that comes from living and contributing to a small and growing community. Their home was warm and comfortable. In Chicago the family loses all sense of community. They live in a cold and uncomfortable apartment. Any security and pride derived from being leading citizens of a small community are lost to the Hausers in Chicago. Although Julia finds the bustle and excitement that she so craves, there is strife within the family. Their son wishes to return to Nebraska, and Julia's husband is a broken man, lost both financially and socially without the support system built up over his many years in Nebraska. The novel ends with Julia achieving her long sought-after goal, but it comes with a heavy price. The conclusion indicates Walker's ambivalence about movement and the public's fascination with speed.

This tug-of-war between the excitement and possibilities available elsewhere and the sense of dispossession that follows constant movement appear throughout Walker's novels. She has some characters leaving the East and moving to the West and others returning to the East or to the West, all the while continuously debating the pros and cons of each landscape and lifestyle. Walker must have considered these issues, particularly during her decades in Montana. Although these were her most productive years, the compromises required for active participation in the life and growth of the new West and the possible outcomes of these changes were never far from her mind.

Her own private writings indicate her ambivalence about movement. In one particularly candid essay still retained by the Schemm family, "Vermont Exiles," she discusses other displaced New Englanders she meets in Montana. In this, Walker writes:

> We exiles from Vermont have one curious quality in common. We would not go back if we could, not to live, we explain always in a certain tone of voice, and yet we cherish the fancy as though it were truth that no place in the world appeals to us with quite the poignance of Vermont. Perhaps it is the truth.
>
> This, be it fancy or truth, gives us a sense of nostalgia when we contemplate it and etches a delicate shadow in our minds. We are like any emigrant remembering the old country. We are quick to adopt the larger, easier ways of living in cities farther west yet always with a secret scorn in them. "Back in Vermont," we say to ourselves, or if we find a person to listen, to others, you'd have no more thought

> of adjusting a thermostat to get your heat than of flying; you went out to the woodshed and got some wood. And we have, someway, a feeling of superiority because of our knowledge of Vermont life.
>
> There are many of us. It is no wonder that the hills are empty of people and the census of the four corners of Vermont shows a decrease when you think how far we have spread. "There is energy in those hills" and an accent so like old Alden Walker's, our great uncle, creeps into our voice that even we are aware of it. I am only a third generation Vermont exile. I knew Vermont only in the long, lazy days of childhood yet there is a nostalgic drawing toward the Vermont of the ancestors in me, too, and when I go back a certain peace settles upon me that I find nowhere else. I gloat in being possessed once again by those low hills and small, quiet rooms and a brook so old it will always make me aware of my merest youth. Vermont is a blood heritage just as is that of Daniel Boone or the proud Spanish blood of many Californians and we Americans can little afford to toss up any heritage without valuing it. No maturity of thought or culture will ever come from the "Unpossessed". The traditions of the unpossessed are written in the dust that settles on the tops of the New York City skyscrapers but like that dust they blow away. We Vermonters sometimes seem smug, but the smugness is only an outer moss of seeming. There is a humility like a rib of granite underneath.

Although there is no date on "Vermont Exiles," given its subject matter, it would seem that it was written some time during the author's years in Montana. Many of her novels compare "westering" versus "eastering" and the "rural" versus the "urban," but nowhere are the author's own feelings on these concepts expressed more clearly than in "Vermont Exiles."

It is noteworthy that in this essay Walker uses the image of the dust on a New York City skyscraper as a metaphor for the lost lives of the modern dispossessed. Not only does this metaphor imply urbanization's role in these feelings of dispossession, the skyscraper is also a vibrant symbol of the future, of man's ingenuity, and of the increasing mechanization of our society. By choosing this image, she indicates the presence of differences not only between the East and West and the rural and the urban but also between the handmade and the machine-made.

Lyman Converse in *The Quarry* is one of Walker's characters who best captures the complexity of the issues she raises in "Vermont Exiles"—the concern with movement and mechanization and the relationship between things rooted in place and those things that soar in modern times. In this story, modern life leaves Lyman behind, much as the war did. Lyman was too young to participate in the Civil War and too young, the text indicates, to get that taste of freedom that his older brothers had once they left the green hills of Vermont. When Lyman's older brother, Dan, returns to Vermont from the war, the family fully anticipates that he will fall back into life in Vermont and take over the family quarry. However, Dan surprises and disappoints his family by announcing soon after his arrival his imminent departure for the West (101). Somehow, the indication here is that the movement from his Vermont hills caused by the war completely changed Dan's and many others' futures, values, and goals. Dan leaves home when Lyman is still an adolescent, and for the rest of his life Lyman will only share snippets of this other life his brother and others experience in the West as he continues to work away in a dying enterprise in the appropriately named Painesville, Vermont.

Regarding those who left New England, Hugo writes in her mother's biography: "According to Mother, those who moved out west at the time showed 'gumption'. She mentioned more than once to us that those who stayed in New England had lacked gumption, a notion she would pursue in *The Quarry*" (12). Certainly, Walker pursued this subject in *The Quarry*, and it is also possible that she characterizes Lyman, the New Englander who stayed behind, as an individual who thought he lacked "gumption" but who, in reality, did not.

New England lost much of its economic and social prominence after the Civil War. The same technology that propelled the war efforts brought an end to many small New England businesses, soapstone quarries included. By the end of the novel, the family's quarry business has all but ceased to exist. With the development of cement and other industrial products, no market remains for a business that sustained Lyman's family for generations. The novel traces the family from the height of their economic prosperity before the Civil War to their reduced means by the time of the outbreak of World War I, depicted by Lyman's wife, begrudgingly renting out rooms in their family home to summer tourists for extra cash.

At the height of his desperation, feeling that the world has left him behind and that the movement into the twentieth century has not been his, Lyman makes a trip up to his abandoned quarry. As he travels, he thinks to himself: "How had it happened? [. . .] [H]ow had it come about that he had become merely an observer of life? Except for his brief adventure at college and his trip out West, it seemed to him that he had been looking on at life, observing" (314). In his carriage, he reflects on what he sees as the meaninglessness of his life compared to the other more active men in the Converse family. At this point, he actually considers drowning himself in the quarry, flooded with water since the pumps stopped (334). However, Lyman does not kill himself. As he is about to jump into the water of the old quarry, his childhood friend, Easy, appears with a bucket of berries. Throughout the novel, Easy has represented the alternative approach to Lyman Converse's modern cravings. Easy, the freed slave, appears unencumbered by Lyman's sources of despair. Ironically, of the two characters, it is Lyman who has been portrayed as enslaved throughout the novel. Easy is the character seemingly privileged to live a new life of freedom. When Lyman was a boy, Easy taught him about humility, honesty, and friendship. At the end of the novel, Easy, now an old man, again teaches Lyman about the true values in life.

When Lyman asks, "Don't you wonder sometimes, Easy, what good our lives have been?" the narrator adds that Easy takes a long time responding and then says, "No, Lyman, that don't worry me. Our lives got a sweet taste in the mouth most o' the time" (338).

Examining this dialogue, it is apparent that Lyman's question comes from an ethos steeped in the traditions of the Protestant work ethic. When he asks, "What good our lives have been?" the implied question is, "Of what economic worth have they been?" This is the counting, the efficiency, and the productivity—seemingly "the movement and soaring" that measures modern life. What Lyman literally asks Easy is, "What have we produced? How many miles have we traveled? What have we contributed?" Lyman's despair is also reminiscent of Henry David Thoreau's observation found in his famous quote: "The mass of men lead lives of quite desperation. What is called resignation is confirmed desperation" (5). Easy, however, will not count and will not be entangled, either in his thoughts or in his words, in the system of productivity, measured movement, and commodification that enslaved him as a child. He answers the question from a different plateau, not from a world that counts but instead from a slower and more sensuous world. He simply but carefully says, "No . . . Our lives got a sweet taste in the mouth most o' the time." Akin to Henry David Thoreau, Easy encourages a life of physicality. In fact, Thoreau, in the chapter "The Ponds" in *Walden*, and Walker, in the scene between Easy and Lyman in *The Quarry*, employ the same metaphor of sweet berries to emphasize this point. Thoreau writes, "If you would know the flavor of huckleberries, ask the cow-boy or the partridge. It is a vulgar error to suppose that you have tasted huckleberries who never plucked them" (116). Similarly, prior to his response to Lyman, Easy pops some berries in his mouth that he has just picked from a nearby bush.

In *The Quarry* readers again find evidence of the mixed feelings Walker's characters convey while participating in the activities that mark modern times. It is noteworthy that Converse's brother, who moved out west, found an early death by hanging after falling in with the wrong group. His end could be read as an indication of the author's wariness of departing from a traditional way of life.

If *The Quarry* were Walker's only novel, her readers might conclude that she held firm to some modernists' distrust of speed, movement, and change. However, these same issues appear several other times in her novels with very different outcomes for their characters. For instance, in both *Winter Wheat* and *The Curlew's Cry*, readers are again confronted by issues surrounding American movement: of east versus west, rural versus urban, and mechanized versus handmade, of the New Englander moving west and the Westerner moving east.

In *Winter Wheat* Ellen's father exhibits mixed feelings about his physically demanding and culturally isolated life in Montana as opposed to the more genteel life that he left behind in Vermont. But when his moment of crisis comes and he travels away from Montana, alone and during Christmas, for a trip back east to help his sister and to also sort out his own feelings, his wife tells her daughter about his other aborted trips back East and recalls that twice before he had left Montana but returned without having made the journey. In this section of the novel, the tension is heightened by the question of whether or not Ben will return to the West. At one point, Anna conjectures, "But this time I guess he go all the way" (222). Ben's absence and the underlying tension it causes create a heaviness that hangs over the women's quiet Christmas. The economic deterioration of the lives of New Englanders and the financial insecurity of Ben's family are noted in his one letter home, but there is still uneasiness in the household and an indication that the women believe that he still might choose a life in the East, despite the negativity. As the days pass and the tension builds, readers sense an insecurity lying at the heart of American households that is caused by this newfound mobility to shift back and forth across the country by train. However, this tension subsides when Ben surprises Ellen and her mother by arriving back in Montana earlier than planned. It is clear, even with as little as is said, that he has made his choice and come to his peace with life in the West. For instance, when Ellen asks, "Did you have a good time Dad?" he responds by saying, slowly, "Well, it was a satisfaction [. . .]. I'm sorry, but I couldn't have done anything else" (234). This is the last mention of the East in *Winter Wheat*, and readers are left to believe that the Webbs are settled, even though the narrative leaves an underlying residue and worry concerning the instability of community and home.

Although the physical journeys in *The Curlew's Cry* are from West to East rather than East to West, as they are in *Winter Wheat*, similar concerns emanate from this constant movement across the country and also extenuate this novel's tension. In *The Curlew's Cry*, Pamela Lacey, born in Montana, travels and then resides in New York. In Pamela's case, she seems even more alien and displaced in New York than Ben Webb does in Montana. Despite the social stigma and personal pain involved in her subsequent move, Pamela returns to the West alone and eventually divorces her husband. The implication in the novel is that Pamela's divorce is precipitated more by her feelings of alienation stemming from living in New York than from any particular animosity between Pamela and her well-meaning but thoroughly eastern husband. The narrator is careful in this novel not to oversimplify the results of this character's decision. Pamela does not simply return to her family's ranch and happily watch the sun set in the West. In fact, the metaphor in the novel's title—the curlew's cry—clearly captures the complexity of Pamela's choice of remaining in one location and continuing in a chosen lifestyle.

In the notes Walker kept while writing *The Curlew's Cry*, readers find further evidence of her ambivalence about life in the West. In a journal entry she paraphrases a quote Ray West made concerning Wallace Stegner: "recognized West no longer scene for heroic action" (qtd. in Hugo: 189). The implication in this quote is that although Walker and her family embraced western life and bought a rustic cabin in the Rattlesnake Range and enjoyed their acreage on the Missouri river, riding horses, hiking, and working toward building a community in Montana, they were never deluded by the western dream or myth of any possibility for heroic self-creation and were also wary of those individuals who continued to be. Furthermore, Walker the author would not re-create a world in her fiction that she personally did not believe existed, such as the epic West, a place bigger than life and with room enough for solitary heroes and self-creation. Pamela's road home to Montana is a difficult journey because the solitude of the West takes its toll on its residents— an isolation that the lonely cry of the curlew captures.

In turning her back on the mythic West, Walker's approach to the West and re-creation of its characters and their lives have much in common with Wallace Stegner's work. The two writers' lives and movements have great similarities as well. It is not surprising that Walker's journals contain comments about Stegner. Both are best known for their writing about the American West. Walker has long been celebrated as a Montana novelist, while Stegner is often referred to by reviewers as "the dean of western writers" (Benson 125). But while both writers are best remembered for their novels set in the West, both also returned to (and seemed to prefer) New England after many years of life in the West. In fact, Jackson J. Benson, Stegner's biographer, reports in an essay in *Down by the Lemonade Springs* how surprised he was to learn that "this writer, who had written with such affection about so many western locales, told me if he had to choose between his house in California and his place in Vermont, he would choose Vermont" (122). Similarly, upon her husband's death in 1955, Walker wasted no time in selling the family home at Beaverbank and moving back East. This certainly cannot be read solely as a rejection of the West. Her reasons for going were many. Staying in the big Montana house with so many happy memories seemed pointless to her, particularly with her children almost all off at school. She also explained to her family that with her husband gone, she didn't want to be referred to by Great Falls neighbors as "the widow." The possibility of a position teaching English back east at Wells College in New York was also an impetus for her departure. However, her move back east might also be read as a return to a more familiar landscape and some deeper roots than those she may have sensed she held in the dry Montana soil, despite their years of cultivation. Again, upon her retirement from teaching at Wells in 1968, Walker moved right back to her family's summer home in Grafton, Vermont. This move brought her full circle to her childhood roots and to a place that presumably was welcoming and comforting. If not for failing health in her last years and the necessity of a residence closer to family members back out west, there is every indication that she would have stayed in Grafton permanently.

The irony in Walker's movements across the country is that her most productive and happiest years were those in Montana. Nine of her thirteen novels were published in the twenty-two years she lived in the West. On a more personal level, her daughter reflects, "I knew with a sense of underlying happiness how Mother delighted in the living at Beaverbank"—the family acreage and home on the Missouri River (161). However, like many other Westerners and writers, she moved back East. Perhaps Walker's feelings in her latter years were again similar to Stegner's. In *American Places*, Stegner reflected on life in New England and wrote: "[Vermont] has watched humanity go by, and has recovered from the visit" (qtd. in Benson, *Lemonade Springs*: 126). Perhaps in his later years, Stegner was disappointed in what he saw as the greed and exploitation of the western landscape and what he referred to as the public's "get rich quick attitude"—a subject that he explored in many of his works, particularly in his novel *The Big Rock Candy Mountain*. In contrast, the return to the dense forest and growth in

New England was a comfort to Stegner. Furthermore, he found the people in Vermont to be "neighborly, helpful and quite astonishingly tolerant of difference and eccentricity. They judge[d] a person primarily by how he or she works" (Stegner, *American Places* 40). Additionally, for a writer whose sense of homelessness haunted and informed most of his fiction, the deep roots of Vermont must have fulfilled a gnawing emptiness that no other place could. So too was the case, perhaps, for Walker.

One of the best examples of Walker's exploration of belonging and home is found in *The Southwest Corner*. In this novella, the elderly Marcia Elder is presented as a somewhat eccentric New England character. Despite her advanced years and the fact that all the hillside farms around her have been abandoned, she is determined to live out her remaining days in her family's farmhouse. With her advancing age and diminishing strength, the tension of the novel is based on her search to find a way to stay. Her quest requires a re-creation of some sense of community. From the very start of the story, Marcia knows that only through a cooperative and mutually beneficial social arrangement can her hopes of living and preserving the family farmstead come to fruition because she is no longer well enough to stay on in the farm by herself. At the end of the novella, Marcia finds a young partner to come and share her farm, and readers sense that in this, there is the much needed infusion of new life that will continue to nurture the deep roots of Marcia's heritage.

Upon her return to her familiar old New England in 1968, the author reflected in her personal journal entries on the new chapter of her life she was about to begin: "Now I shall begin to make my own life here—on this summer day of Sunday afternoon stillness [. . .] I've got to go deeper. I've lived largely at the surface" (qtd. in Hugo: 245). When she writes, "I've got to go deeper" and "I've lived largely at the surface," readers again get a sense not only of this search for deep roots but also of Walker's implication that much of her earlier life has been a superficial toehold.

Further clarification of Walker's feeling may lie in the words of one of her unpublished essays on Vermont titled "A Child Beside a Pool." In this, the author recalls a youngster with her face down to the clear water and notes that "it is here in this stream I first touched mysticism, was caught up from reality . . . for one long childhood moment" (qtd. in Hugo: 4–5). This entry is exceptional for Walker's use of the word "mysticism" and for her reference to leaving reality behind. Walker seldom mentions such concepts as mysticism, and its rare appearance in this context is revealing. Perhaps the water that she describes tumbling over the stones beneath the Saxtons River outside her Grafton farmhouse metaphorically captures all Walker viewed as both the static and dynamic in her life. Additionally, perhaps the author indicates in this passage that only in a place where she felt truly at home and rooted was she comfortable enough to touch something beyond the moving and busy world.

Because of this constant tug-of-war between belonging and moving, modernists have often been characterized as "outsiders." Much has been written on the value to a writer of becoming or remaining "an outsider." For instance, in *Ernest Hemingway and the Expatriate Movement*, Matthew Bruccoli quotes Gertrude Stein in her essay "An American and France" to illustrate the necessity of being "an outsider":

> Artists thus need two homelands—the one from which they come and the one that allows them to live in isolation: "It is very natural that everyone who makes anything inside themselves [. . .] does naturally have to have two civilizations. They have to have the civilization that makes them and the civilization that has nothing to do with them." Only through this extreme detachment can artistic expression occur, for "if you are you in your civilization you are apt to mix yourself up too much with your civilization but when it is another civilization [. . .] you have the freedom inside yourself." (qtd. in Bruccoli: 63)

Concerning modernist alienation and Wallace Stegner's writing, Jackson J. Benson also notes that "out of this background" of continuous movement and displacement "we can see . . . a concern for the effects of cultural transplantation, a concern for questions about what holds a family together and what drives it apart, and a concern for having roots, both in family and place, and knowing about them" (Benson, *Lemonade Springs* 130).

It might be said that journeys and movement were integral to the creation and subject matter of modernist writing, but an underlying concern was the journey home, wherever that resting place might be. For Walker, that place seemed to be somewhere deeper, a place where she first sensed "mysticism"—Vermont. Many characters in her novels also had to make this journey homeward, but they also grew from the displacement and movement they experienced. In *Spaces of the Mind*, Elaine Jahner includes a detailed discussion of Ellen Webb's movement and concomitant growth in *Winter Wheat*. Jahner notes:

> *Winter Wheat* covers the span of two growing seasons, two times of latent development for what grows in early spring. Ellen spends the first winter at the University of Minnesota in Minneapolis, where she learns to look at Montana from the *outside in*. She also begins the process of trying to write about her Montana life, so we can follow her own attempts to understand her life as narrative. She spends the second year at home because she agrees to teach in a one-room rural school; that reimmersion in a life she thought she was leaving teaches her to see the place from the *inside out*. With that turnabout, she grasps how much she had previously missed about the emotional economy of her family, and that fundamental revision gradually gets linked to an understanding of how the setting of Montana has set up conditions for communication or the lack thereof among family members. (141; italics added)

Moreover, Jahner explains how Ellen (much akin to her author) will create a new language and develop a greater understanding of linguistic signifiers resulting from her journey away from home. In fact, Ellen feels compelled to create the narrative of her family and their lives using the metaphor of winter wheat, in much the same way as modernists re-created an understanding of their world with a self-conscious re-creation and manipulation of linguistic tools in their fiction. In Ellen Webb's fictional character, Walker re-creates the modernist who moves from the comforts of a traditional setting and a world with language to a world where narrative reinvention is integral to understanding and acceptance. If, as Jahner explains, Ellen's growth occurs through her psychological and physical movement from the inside to the outside, many modernists accomplish a similar growth through movement.

Notably, in *A Piece of the World*, the last novel Walker was to see published during her lifetime, she once again focused her text on issues of movement, displacement, alienation, and life in Vermont. In this novel modern life and enterprise take an almost absurd turn when a developer undertakes a project to move a huge, erratic boulder, found hidden in the hills above the village, down to the public square in an attempt to create a tourist attraction: a story sadly reminiscent of tourists chipping away at pieces of Plymouth Rock for souvenirs before the U.S. Park Service protected it from the public.

In this novel, teenaged Calder Bailey has been sent back to New England from California to spend the summer with her grandmother. Calder sympathetically takes up the battle to maintain the boulder in its current resting place while she waits and attempts to come to terms with her parents' divorce and their decisions about new residences. Calder draws a metaphorical connection between the boulder's rightful place and her own. The battle to maintain the boulder in its original location is unsuccessful and the out-of-town developer has the boulder broken into four pieces, transported into town, and cemented back together. Many of the townspeople claim that they cannot even see the cement cracks, but Calder and her friends see and feel them.

In a letter to her father, Calder tries to describe cheerfully how the way the rock is put back together "really is a miracle"

(216), writing with a childish and somewhat false exuberance about both the rock and her future prospects. Her words in the first paragraphs of the letter to her father reveal much more about her true feelings:

> When Mr. Cooley told Mother the rock is called an erratic boulder in geology books, she said that was perfect for a Vermont village because there are so many erratic people in one. And Mr. Tom said, "Aren't we all?" I liked that. Another geology book's name for a glacial boulder is lost rock, because it is separated from the parent rock. [. . .]
>
> Mr. Cooley, my geologist friend, says it has brought the wilderness into the village. I think it must feel trapped down here and be hoping for another glacier to carry it away and smash all the houses that wall it in [. . .]. (216)

Again, in this conclusion, readers find indications of Walker's own complex thoughts on movement and the future—a combination of her forced optimism, her knowledge and acceptance of the inevitability of change, and her cautionary stance concerning humanity's desire to constantly move itself—and even mountains—and the price to be paid for such ambitions.

Whether movement or displacement is to be viewed positively or negatively, spiritually or intellectually, Ralph Waldo Emerson believed transition was infused with power, as did many subsequent modernists. This transition, ubiquitous in modern life, fueled Walker's fiction, and today, her novels remain relevant and infused with the energy of compromise and the language of movement: her modernism.

Works Cited

The American Heritage Center at the University of Wyoming in Laramie lists the following materials under the name of Mildred Walker Schemm: original hardcover versions of her novels; manuscripts or galley proofs for all published novels; handwritten notebooks for background work on each of the novels; the author's business correspondence; original book reviews; news clippings; copies of translations of selected novels into nine languages; personal journals; and private papers and letters. (Accession Number: 1393-01-08-24)

Adams, Henry. *The Education of Henry Adams.* 1918. Boston: Houghton Mifflin, 1961.

Adorno, Theodor. *The Culture Industry.* 1981. London: Routledge, 2002.

Anderson, Sherwood. *Winesburg, Ohio.* 1919. Introd. Malcolm Cowley. New York: Milestone Editions, 1960.

Ardis, Ann L. *New Women, New Novels: Feminism and Early Modernism.* New Brunswick NJ: Rutgers UP, 1990.

Ardis, Ann L., and Leslie Lewis, eds. *Womens' Experience of Modernity, 1875–1945.* Baltimore: Johns Hopkins UP, 2003.

Austin, Diana. "Over the Frontier and into the Darkness with Stevie Smith: War, Gender, and Identity." *Challenging Modernism: New Readings in Literature and Culture, 1914–45.* Ed. Stella Dean. Burlington VT: Ashgate Press, 2002. 35–53.

Baker, Carlos. *Ernest Hemingway: A Life Story*. New York: Bantam, 1968.

Benson, Jackson. *Down by the Lemonade Springs: Essays on Wallace Stegner*. 1995. Reno: University of Nevada Press, 2001.

———. *Wallace Stegner: His Life and Work*. New York: Viking, 1996.

Berman, Marshall. *All That Is Solid Melts Into Air: The Experience of Modernity*. New York: Simon and Schuster, 1982.

Bevis, William W. Introduction. *Ten Tough Trips: Montana Writers and the West*. Seattle: U of Washington P, 1990.

Blew, Mary Clearman. Introduction. *The Curlew's Cry*. 1955. By Mildred Walker. Lincoln: U of Nebraska P, 1994. 1–7.

———. "Mother Lodge." *Bone Deep in Landscape: Writing, Reading, and Place*. U of Oklahoma P, 1999. 100–110.

Bluemel, Kristin. *Experimenting on the Borders of Modernism: Dorothy Richardson's Pilgrimage*. Athens GA: U of Georgia P, 1997.

Bourdieu, Pierre. *The Field of Cultural Production: Essays on Art and Literature*. Ed. and introd. Randal Johnson. New York: Columbia UP, 1993.

Bradbury, Malcolm and James McFarlane, eds. *Modernism, 1890–1930: A Guide to European Literature*. 1976. London: Penguin, 1991.

Bradford, William. *Of Plymouth Plantation, 1620–1647*. Ed. and introd. Francis Murphy. New York: Modern Library, 1981.

Bruccoli, Matthew J. and Richard Layman, eds. *Ernest Hemingway and the Expatriate Modernist Movement—Literary Topics*. Vol. 2. Detroit: A Manly, Inc. Book—Gale Group, 2000.

Bryan, Sharon. Introduction. *The Body of a Young Man*. 1960. By Mildred Walker. U of Nebraska P, 1997. vii–xi.

———, ed. Introduction. *Where We Stand: Women Poets on Literary Tradition*. New York: Norton, 1993. vii–xiv.

Budbill, David. Introduction. *The Brewers' Big Horses*. 1940. By Mildred Walker. Lincoln: U of Nebraska P, 1996. vii–xiv.

———. Introduction. *Dr. Norton's Wife*. 1939. By Mildred Walker. Lincoln: U of Nebraska P, 1994. vii–xvii.

Cather, Willa. *My Ántonia*. 1918. New York: Houghton, 1987.

———. *One of Ours*. 1922. New York: Houghton, 1987.

Childs, Peter. *Modernism: The New Critical Idiom*. London: Routledge, 2000.

Clark, Suzanne. *Sentimental Modernism: Women Writers and the Revolution of the Word*. Bloomington: Indiana UP, 1991.

Collier, Patrick. "T.S. Eliot in the Journalistic Struggle." *Challenging Modernism: New Readings in Literature and Culture, 1914–45*. Ed. Stella Deen. Burlington VT: Ashgate, 2002. 187–212.

Comer, Krista. *Landscapes of the New West: Gender and Geography in Contemporary Women's Writing*. Chapel Hill: U of North Carolina P, 1999.

Conrad, Joseph. "Heart of Darkness." 1902. *The Portable Conrad*. Ed. and introd. Morton Dauwen Zabel. New York: Viking Press, 1975. 490–605.

Deen, Stella, ed. *Challenging Modernism: New Readings in Literature and Culture, 1914–45*. Burlington VT: Ashgate, 2002.

Egan, Ken, Jr. *Hope and Dread in Montana Literature*. Reno: U of Nevada P, 2003.

Eliot, T. S. "The Waste Land." *Norton Anthology of American Literature: Between the Wars, 1914–1945*. Eds. Nina Baym et al. 6th ed. Vol. D. New York: Norton, 2003. 1430–43.

Emerson, Ralph Waldo. *Complete Works of Ralph Waldo Emerson*. Ed. Joel Myerson. New York: AMS Press, 1979.

Eysteinsson, Astradur. *The Concept of Modernism*. Ithaca: Cornell UP, 1990.

Faulkner, William. *As I Lay Dying*. 1930. New York: Modern Library, 1967.

———. *The Portable Faulkner*. 1946. Ed. Malcolm Cowley. London: Penguin, 2003.

Felski, Rita. Afterward. *Women's Experience of Modernity, 1875–1945*. Eds. Ann L. Ardis and Leslie Lewis. Baltimore: John Hopkins UP, 2003. 290–99.

Fetterley, Judith, and Marjorie Pryse, eds. Introduction. *American Women Regionalists: A Norton Anthology*. New York: Norton, 1992. xi–xx.

Fitzgerald, F. Scott. *The Great Gatsby*. 1925. New York: Scribner's, 1953.

Forster, E. M. *Aspects of the Novel*. 1927. New York: Harcourt, 1955

———. *Howard's End*. 1910. London: Edward and Arnold, 1973.

Gambrell, Alice. *Women Intellectuals, Modernism, and Difference: Transatlantic Culture, 1919–1945*. Cambridge: Cambridge UP, 1997.

Gillespie, Diane F. "Introduction: Dorothy Richardson." *The Gender of Modernism: A Critical Anthology*. Ed. Bonnie Kime Scott. Bloomington: Indiana UP, 1990. 393–99.

Giroux, Robert. Introduction. *Medical Meeting*. 1955. By Mildred Walker. Lincoln: U of Nebraska P, 1994. vii–x.

Gloss, Molly. "Mildred Walker: A Portrait." *The Burnside Reader*. Ed. Bob Gloss. Portland OR: Powell's City of Books, Spring 1995. 41–46.

Hanscombe, Gillian, and Virginia L. Smyers. *Writing for Their Lives: The Modernist Women, 1919–1940*. London: The Women's Press, 1987.

Hemingway, Ernest. "The Art of the Short Story." *New Critical Approaches to the Short Stories of Ernest Hemingway*. Ed. Jackson J. Benson. Durham NC: Duke UP, 1991. 1–13.

———. "Big Two-Hearted River." *In Our Time*. 1925. New York: Scribner's, 1953. 175–212.

———. *Death in the Afternoon*. New York: Scribner's, 1932.

———. *Ernest Hemingway, Selected Letters, 1917–1961*. Ed. Carlos Baker. New York: Scribner's, 1981.

Hill, Marylu. *Mothering Modernity: Feminism, Modernism, and the Maternal Muse*. New York: Garland, 1999.

Hugo, Ripley. *Writing for Her Life: The Novelist Mildred Walker*. Lincoln: U of Nebraska P, 2003.

———. Introduction. *The Quarry*. 1947. By Mildred Walker. Lincoln: U of Nebraska P, 1995. vii–xii.

———. Telephone interviews. 2003–5.

———. "Video of Mildred Walker in Montana." From Schemm family collection. N.d.

Jahner, Elaine. *Spaces of the Mind: Narrative and Community in the American West*. Lincoln: U of Nebraska P, 2004.

James, Henry. *The Art of the Novel*. 1934. Foreword R .W. B Lewis. Introd. R. P. Blackmuir. Boston: Northeastern UP, 1984.

———. *Daisy Miller*. 1878. *Great Short Works of Henry James*. Introd. Dean Fowler. New York: Harper, 1966. 1–55.

———. *The Golden Bowl*. New York: Scribner's, 1904.

Joyce, James. *Ulysses*. New York: The Modern Library, 1934.

Kasson, John F. *Civilizing the Machine: Technology and Republican Values in America, 1776–1900*. New York: Hill and Wang, 1999.

Kittredge, William and Annick Smith, eds. *The Last Best Place: A Montana Anthology*. Seattle: U of Washington P, 1988.

Kristeva, Julia. *The Kristeva Reader*. Ed. Toril Moi. New York: Columbia UP, 1986.

Kuna, Franz. "The Janus-faced Novel: Conrad, Musil, Kafka, Mann." *Modernism, 1890–1930: A Guide to European Literature*. Eds. Malcolm Bradbury and James McFarlane. London: Penguin, 1991. 443–52.

Lamont, Victoria. "Cattle Branding and the Traffic in Women in Early Twentieth-Century Westerns by Women." *Legacy* 22.1 (2005): 30–46.

Lilienfeld, Jane. "Introduction to Willa Cather." *The Gender of Modernism: A Critical Anthology*. Ed. Bonnie Kime Scott. Indianapolis: Indiana UP, 1990. 46–53.

Lodge, David. "The Language of Modernist Fiction: Metaphor and Metonymy." *Modernism, 1890–1930: A Guide to European Literature*. Eds. Malcolm Bradbury and James McFarlane. London: Penguin, 1991. 481–96.

Maclean, Norman. *A River Runs Through It, and Other Stories*. Chicago: U of Chicago P, 1976.

McGurl, Mark. *The Novel Art: Elevations of American Fiction after Henry James*. Princeton: Princeton UP, 2001.

McNamer, Deidre. “Exquisite Solitude: The Life and Writing of Mildred Walker Schemm ’26.” *The Express* (Winter 2001): 4–9.

———. Introduction. *Unless the Wind Turns*. 1941. By Mildred Walker. Lincoln: U of Nebraska P, 1996. vii–xiii.

Meade, Marion. *Bobbed Hair and Bathtub Gin: Writers Running Wild in the Twenties*. Orlando FL: Harcourt, 2004

Meisel, Perry. *The Myth of the Modern: A Study in British Literature and Criticism after 1850*. New Haven: Yale UP, 1987.

Middleton, Jo Ann. *Willa Cather’s Modernism: A Study of Style and Technique*. Rutherford NJ: Fairleigh Dickinson UP, 1990.

“Mildred Walker Schemm: 1905–1998.” *Literature Resource Center*. May 7, 2003. <http://galenet.galegroup.com/servlet/LitRC?c+1&ADVSF1=mildred+walker&ASB2+AND&ASB1 . . . >.

“Mildred Walker: What the Critics Say.” *Nebraska Center for Writers*. May 7, 2003. <http://mockingbird.creighton.edu/ncw/walkcrit.htm>.

Norris, Frank. *The Octopus*. 1901. New York: Doubleday, 1958.

“One Book Montana: Mildred Walker Biographical and Bibliographical Information.” *Montana Center for the Book*. September 19, 2003. <http://www.montanabook.org/bio biblio.htm>.

Pearson, Carmen. “Mildred Walker: An Introduction to Her Life and Work.” *Legacy*. 22.2 (2005): 187–95.

———. “Mildred Walker and Modernism.” Paper presented at the *American Literature Association* Conference. Boston MA. May 2005.

———. “Mildred Walker’s Working Women: In Woods, Wheatfields, and Ranchlands.” Paper presented at the *Association for the Study of Literature and the Environment* Conference. Eugene OR. June 2005.

———. “Montana’s Mixed Marriages as Depicted in Mildred

Walker's *Winter Wheat*." Paper presented at the *Western American Literature Association* Conference. Los Angeles. October 2005.

———. "Nature Informing the Novels of Mildred Walker." Paper presented at the *Western American Literature Association* Conference. Big Sky MT. September 2004.

———. "Resurrecting the Unremembered: A Brief Look into the Novels of Mildred Walker." *South Dakota Review* 41.3 (Fall 2003): 41–51.

———. "A Review of Writing for Her Life: The Novelist Mildred Walker by Ripley Hugo." *Western American Literature* 38.3 (Fall 2003): 317–19.

———, ed. Introduction. *The Orange Tree*. By Mildred Walker. Lincoln: U of Nebraska P, 2006. xi–xv.

Poirier, Richard. "The Difficulties of Modernism and the Modernism of Difficulty." *Humanities in Society* 1 (1978): 271–82.

Putman, Hannah. "A Bumper Crop of Literary Events." *Humanities* 24.5 (Sept.–Oct. 2003): 36–37.

Rainey, Lawrence. "The Cultural Economy of Modernism." *The Cambridge Companion to Modernism*. Ed. Michael Levenson. Cambridge: Cambridge UP, 2003. 33–69.

Richardson, Dorothy. *Pilgrimage*, 1915–38. 4 vols. London: Virago, 1979.

———. *Windows on Modernism: Selected Letters of Dorothy Richardson*. Ed. Gloria G. Fromm. Athens GA: U of Georgia P, 1995.

Rogers, Michael. "Book Reviews: Classic Returns." *Library Journal* 120.20 (Dec. 1995): 165.

Ronald, Ann. "A Montana Maturity." *Reader of the Purple Sage: Essays on Western Writers and Environmental Literature*. Reno: U of Nevada P, 2003. 95–105.

Ruland, Richard and Malcolm Bradbury, eds. *From Puritanism to Postmodernism: A History of American Literature*. London: Penguin, 1991.

Scott, Bonnie Kime. *Refiguring Modernism: The Women of 1928*. Bloomington: Indiana UP, 1995.

———, ed. *The Gender of Modernism: A Critical Anthology*. Bloomington: Indiana UP, 1990.

Schwartz, Sanford. "The Postmodernity of Modernism." *The Future of Modernism*. Ed. Hugh Witemeyer. Ann Arbor: U of Michigan P, 2000. 33–47.

Smith, Annick. Introduction. *Fireweed*. 1934. By Mildred Walker. Lincoln: U of Nebraska P, 1994. vii–xv.

Stein, Gertrude. *The Autobiography of Alice B. Toklas*. New York: Harcourt Brace, 1933.

———. "How Writing is Written." *The Gender of Modernism: A Critical Anthology*. Ed. Bonnie Kime Scott. Bloomington: Indiana UP, 1990. 488–94.

Steinbeck, John. *The Grapes of Wrath*. 1939. New York: Penguin, 1980.

———. *Journal of a Novel: The East of Eden Letters*. 1969. New York: Penguin, 1990.

———. "The Red Pony." 1945. *The Pearl/The Red Pony*. London: Penguin Books, 1986.

———. *Travels With Charley*. 1962. Introd. Jay Parini. New York: Penguin, 1997.

Stegner, Wallace. *The Big Rock Candy Mountain*. 1943. Lincoln: U of Nebraska P, 1983.

———. *Crossing to Safety*. New York: Random House, 1987.

Stegner, Wallace, and Page Stegner. *American Places*. Moscow ID: U of Idaho P, 1983.

Swander, Mary. Introduction. *Light from Arcturus*. 1935. By Mildred Walker. Lincoln: U of Nebraska P, 1995. vii–xii

Thoreau, Henry David. *Walden and Civil Disobedience*. Ed. Owen Thomas. New York: Norton, 1966.

Twain, Mark. *Adventures of Huckleberry Finn: Complete Text with Introduction, Historical Contexts, Critical Essays*. Ed. Susan K. Harris. Boston: Houghton Mifflin, 2000.

Wagner-Martin, Linda. *The American Novel, 1914–1945: Twayne's*

Critical History of the Novel. Boston: G. K. Hall & Co.-Twayne Publishers, 1990.

Walker, Mildred. *The Body of a Young Man*. 1960. Introd. Sharon Bryan. Lincoln: U of Nebraska P, 1997.

———. *The Brewers' Big Horses*. 1940. Introd. David Budbill. Lincoln: U of Nebraska P, 1996.

———. *The Curlew's Cry*. 1955. Introd. Mary Clearman Blew. Lincoln: U of Nebraska P, 1994.

———. *Dr. Norton's Wife*. 1938. Introd. David Budbill. Lincoln: U of Nebraska P, 1994.

———. *Fireweed*. 1934. Introd. Annick Smith. Lincoln: U of Nebraska P, 1994.

———. *If a Lion Could Talk*. 1970. Introd. James Welch. Lincoln: U of Nebraska P, 1995.

———. *Light from Arcturus*. 1935. Introd. Mary Swander. Lincoln: U of Nebraska P, 1995

———. *Medical Meeting*. 1955. Introd. Robert Giroux. Lincoln: U of Nebraska P, 1994.

———. *The Orange Tree*. Ed. and introd. Carmen Pearson. Lincoln: U of Nebraska P, 2006.

———. *A Piece of the World*. 1972. Lincoln: U of Nebraska P, 2001.

———. *The Quarry*. 1947. Introd. David Budbill. Lincoln: U of Nebraska P, 1995.

———. *The Southwest Corner*. 1951. Foreword Mildred Walker. Lincoln: U of Nebraska P, 1995.

———. *Unless the Wind Turns*. 1941. Introd. Deidre NcNamer. Lincoln: U of Nebraska P, 1996.

———. "Vermont Exiles." Unpublished essay. Schemm family private collection. N.d.

———. *Winter Wheat*. 1944. Introd. James Welch. Lincoln: U of Nebraska P, 1992.

Welch, James. Introduction. *If a Lion Could Talk*. 1970. By Mildred Walker. Lincoln: U of Nebraska P, 1995. vii–xiii.

———. Introduction. *Winter Wheat*. 1944. Lincoln: U of Nebraska P, 1992. ix–xiii.

Whitman, Walt. "Song of Myself." 1855. *Walt Whitman: The Complete Poems*. Ed. Francis Murphy. London: Penguin, 1996. 37–124.

Witemeyer, Hugh, ed. *The Future of Modernism*. Ann Arbor: U of Michigan P, 1998.

Woolf, Virginia. *Mrs. Dalloway*. 1925. Foreword Maureen Howard. London: Harcourt, 1981.

———. *A Room of One's Own*. 1929. Foreword Mary Gordon. New York: Harcourt, 1981.

———. *Three Guineas*. 1938. New York: Harcourt Brace Jovanovich, 1966.

———. *To the Lighthouse*. 1927. Foreword Eudora Welty. New York: Harcourt Brace and World, 1964.

Index

www.ingramcontent.com/pod-product-compliance
Lightning Source LLC
Chambersburg PA
CBHW030356100426
42812CB00028B/2738/J

* 9 7 8 0 8 0 3 2 3 7 6 0 5 *